To the climbers
who inspired and influenced me most
during my learning years—
Bobbi Fosberg, Dave Ingersoll,
Greg Murray, and David Secunda

Traditional Lead Climbing

Surviving the Learning Years

Heidi Pesterfield

 WILDERNESS PRESS · BERKELEY, CA

Traditional Lead Climbing: Surviving the Learning Years

1st EDITION September 2002
2nd printing September 2004

Front cover photo copyright © 2002 by Topher Donahue
Back cover photo copyright © 2002 by Bill McChesney
Frontispiece photo copyright © 2002 by Barry Blanchard
Illustrations: Tami Knight
Instructional photos: Lisa Deering
Cover and book design: Jaan Hitt
Technical editor: Jeff Achey

ISBN 0-89997-255-1
UPC 7-19609-97255-6

Manufactured in the United States of America

♻ Printed on recycled paper

Published by: **Wilderness Press**
1200 5th Street
Berkeley, CA 94710
(800) 443-7227; FAX (510) 558-1696
info@wildernesspress.com
www.wildernesspress.com
Visit our website for a complete listing of our books and for ordering information.

Cover photos: Patience Donahue on Fingerberry Jam in the Bugaboos, British Columbia *(front);*
                  Catherine Davis at Donner Summit, California *(back)*
Frontispiece: Mark Wilford in the St. Elias Range, Alaska
Page xii: Allison Kreutzen at Donner Summit, California *(photo by Bill McChesney)*

Safety Notice
Although Wilderness Press and the author have made every attempt to ensure that the information in this book is accurate at press time, they are not responsible for any loss, damage, injury, or inconvenience that may occur as a result of using this book. You are responsible for your own safety and health while climbing. The fact that a technique is described in this book does not mean it is safe for you. The information contained here is no substitute for professional advice or training. Always check local conditions and know your own limitations.

Library of Congress Cataloging-in-Publication Data
Pesterfield, Heidi, 1962-
Traditional lead climbing : surviving the learning years / Heidi Pesterfield.— 1st ed.
    p. cm.
Includes bibliographical references and index.
ISBN 0-89997-255-1
    1. Rock climbing—Handbooks, manuals, etc. I. Title.
GV200.2 .P47 2002
796.52'23—dc2l

2002069110

CONTENTS

Acknowledgments

Without the gracious assistance and never-ending support of the following individuals, this book would have never been possible: Catherine Davis, Lisa Deering, Doug Robinson, and the staff of Wilderness Press, especially Paul Backhurst, Jaan Hitt and Jannie Dresser.

Additional thanks to: Jeff Achey, Julie Anderson, Brian Bax, Phebe Bell, Maureen Bokeland, Tom Carter, Pete Chasse, Beth Christman, Ann Clemmer, Scott Cosgrove, Mike Davis, Steph Davis, Mimi DeGravelle, Topher Donahue, Patience Donahue, Joe Dolister, Heidi Ettlinger, Chris Falkenstein, Sue Fox, Regan Grillig, Steve Grossman, Jan Holan, Myrna Johnson, Ron Kauk, Bridget Kerr, Allison Kreutzen, Tami Knight, Susie Lancaster, Elaine Lee, Bill McChesney, Billy McCollough, Dave Nettle, The Outdoor Industry Association (previously the Outdoor Recreation Coalition of America), Sarah Patterson, Mike Pennings, Holly Samson, Alia Selke, Hans Standtiemer, Squamish Fish, Peter Thompson, Greg "Thor" Tirdel, and Abby Watkins.

Foreword

I recently saw an ad for "Extreme Banking." It's come to this. The word "extreme" has now become completely, well, bankrupt. But when you think about it, the whole idea was ripe for exploitation from the beginning. It is just freighted with too much of our over-civilized yearning for adventure, for brushing up against totally non-negotiable realities like hard rock and the iron-clad whims of the atmosphere.

Adventure is threatened by such breathless attempts to market it. Why? Because we need it so much. Civilization has gotten too efficient at insulating us from danger, as well as from disease, famine, and pestilence. We would not want the old days back, but along the way we slipped out of touch with some of the fresh, simple delights of being alive, like taking a deep breath of sharp, thin air and really meaning it when we stare at the horizon. We have a deep, almost unconscious urge to return to such immediacy of perception. And an edge of danger helps to keep us in touch.

What is leading? It's stepping out, for sure, getting onto the "sharp end" of the rope. A place where you can get cut. Statistically, falling while leading presents the greatest possibility of being injured while climbing—more dangerous than stonefall, than avalanches and weather, than even rappelling. And yet, climbing on roadside crags, even leading (even trad leading) is statistically safer than driving on the freeway. Or maybe we'd better call that extreme cell phoning.

The big secret is that lead climbing on good rock is surprisingly safe. But that's not how it feels in your gut when you're up there, poised between fear and desire—wanting to pull off a hard move but afraid of the consequences if you don't. Your rational mind figures that a fall with good pro at your knees is merely 6 feet onto a strong rope. But your gut feeling magnifies the possibility—until it quakes with terror—fully convinced of getting mangled on the rocks at the base of the wall. There's always that tension between what your head knows and what your gut feels.

So where's the adventure? It lives and thrives in that gap, the void that yawns between real and apparent danger. *Traditional Lead Climbing* is your ticket to that adventure.

—Doug Robinson
September 2002

Introduction

Ask seasoned rock climbers for the heart of their experience, and they inevitably fix on lead climbing. Life is distilled to pure simplicity when you lead a climb. In this concentrated state, freed of both internal and external distractions, you rediscover your innate ability to experience the present moment. Zen practice never seemed so easy.

Offering yourself to the rock wall above, you navigate up mysterious rock pathways, shifting your focus between motor skills and intellect. Emotions emerge and dissolve, spilling in and out of your consciousness. Angst, fear, confidence, relief — each feeling fades into the past as swiftly as it emerges.

Moving skyward, the objective of taking "the sharp end" becomes more obvious. *Leading* is a game of exploration and discovery. Linking together a chain of holds not visible from the ground, you deftly navigate over bulges and plug your feet and fingers into cracks, all the while looking for ideal protection and rest opportunities. Decisions are made intuitively, as your body embraces a ritual memory entirely its own: placing or forgoing safeguards, resting or not resting, moving right, left, or easing back down to a stance. Your personal orchestration of each individual route as the *leader* is a creative and unique process. No two lead adventures are alike.

Leading gives you opportunities for independence and freedom. Without leading skills, your climbing experience is limited to top-roping or following others. A partnership in which one team member takes every lead cannot be as fulfilling as sharing lead responsibilities.

1

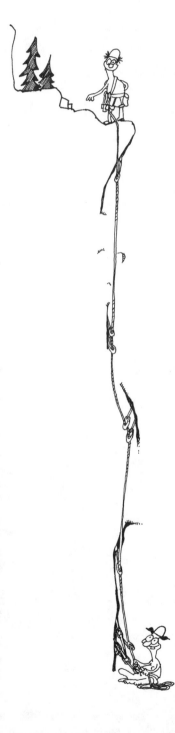

And top-roping opportunities are limited by logistics: arriving only with top-roping gear to explore the celebrated granite cracks of Yosemite Valley, the soaring sandstone towers of southern Utah, or even Bouox's famed limestone pockets in France, is like arriving at Pebble Beach Golf Course with a croquet mallet.

A climber who has just successfully completed a challenging lead possesses an almost ethereal clarity. The disagreeable climber at the base sheds all emotional baggage by the summit. The formerly reticent individual is animated and talkative. Your post-lead "buzz" defines the phrase "on cloud nine" in a way that Merriam or Webster never could. Meet the leader.

Spanning almost two decades, my rock climbing experience features venues that support various styles and methods. Some highlights include bouldering at Hueco Tanks and Fontainbleu, bolt clipping in southern France, free climbing on desert towers, big-wall climbing in Yosemite Valley, and climbing backcountry routes in the Dolomites, the Rockies, the Alps, and the Sierra Nevada mountains in California. While each is a treasured memory, most cherished are the free-climbing experiences that required what is known today as traditional (trad) lead climbing skills.

Trad lead climbing is fundamentally about placing your own protection and anchors. While you may clip an occasional bolt or piton already in place as you lead, you mostly place your own gear: Stoppers, camming devices, Hexes, and other devices, which you set into cracks to create temporary anchors protecting yourself from long falls. As the leader, balancing technical gear skills with physical capabilities while remaining relaxed and focused is your challenge.

Despite its many joys, traditional lead climbing happens to be one of the more dangerous climbing activities. While it offers you adventures aplenty, you enter an arena where risks are extremely high and mistakes unforgiving. Therefore, without expert guidance, learning to lead with gear will be frustrating and could be life-threatening.

I first became motivated to write *Traditional Lead Climbing* when several newcomers asked me to recommend a book that would teach them specifically how to lead with gear. I was certain such a book existed. I erroneously recommended *The Art of Leading*, which turned out to be a short video. After some research I learned that, while the information is available in chapters of several instructional texts, a book had not been written. Now it has.

Another reason to write this book stems from my own challenge learning to lead in Yosemite National Park in 1984—a few years prior to the advent of sport climbing (before gear-leading was referred to as "traditional"). It was a dangerous and frightening undertaking, but I didn't know it at the time. I was young and, like many of my friends, far too consumed in the glory of it all to realize the risks I took. I haphazardly borrowed equipment from (understandably) hesitant friends, and thrashed my way up anything relatively "easy," which, in Yosemite Valley, amounts to a humble smattering of routes you can count on two hands. The instructional information available at this time was sparse, and what was available wasn't as accessible as resources today. Although the copies I owned were obscenely outdated, *Basic Rockcraft* and *Advanced Rockcraft* were my bibles, and probably helped save my butt numerous times.

Today, learning to lead with gear doesn't have to be the dangerous undertaking it was for me. Besides progressive developments in climbing technology, climbers learning to lead in this century have a tremendous amount of instructional information available in frequently updated books, videos, and CD-ROMs, and on the Web. Comprehensive classes offered through guiding services and accredited outdoor programs can provide the new leader with excellent information and hands-on experience in relatively safe environments. Learn all the resources available to you and take advantage of them.

It took a good 10 years before I developed competence as a leader. The skills required are many. Traditional leading is a major undertaking—one significantly more complex than sport climbing, bouldering, or top-roping. This complexity differential is perhaps best illustrated by the analogy of open-ocean (blue-water) sailing to sailing in a bay, where land is always in sight, swells are gentle, and challenges predictable. Like open-ocean sailing, traditional lead climbing involves discovery, adventure, and risk. Without a commitment to learning, your chances of staying alive, let alone truly enjoying yourself, are slim. To embark upon learning this is to commit to a lifetime of education.

It is virtually impossible to gain the skills of an expert trad leader in one season, or even in a year. After 5 years, you'll realize there's even more to learn. And in 10 years, you'll still be making mistakes you thought only beginners make. Accidents can happen even to very experienced and seasoned climbers. Statistics compiled in Canada and the US in 1997 indicate that climbing accidents occur equally among beginner, intermediate, and advanced climbers. This fact should deter you from complacency at each climbing skill level.

How to Use this Book

Traditional Lead Climbing is intended for the intermediate, non-leading rock climber who has a desire to lead with gear. It's also ideal for the climber whose leading experience has been limited to clipping bolts in a sport-climbing setting. **It is not designed to provide instruction for beginner climbers with little or no prior experience.** You should have a basic understanding of standard equipment, as well as experience top-roping or following on real rock. And if you're fresh out of the gym, take some time to get acquainted with a variety of real rock experiences; climbing on plastic only vaguely resembles the real thing. Take it slow, then revisit this book after getting some fresh-air experiences under your belt.

If you're in a hurry to take the sharp end on a traditional route, the guidance in this book may not work for you. But if you embrace the status of beginner and are patient enough to learn this unique and multifaceted craft at a moderate pace, you've got the right book. Just keep in mind the information here *cannot* replace the mentoring of a trained professional. Use the book to supplement other resources.

For learning purposes, this book refers to traditional lead climbing synonymously with gear-leading. Also, the techniques described refer specifically to roped free climbing on rock, unless otherwise stated. More details about the origin of trad free climbing and how it differs from other methods and styles are discussed in Chapter 1. In the context of modern climbing, it is necessary to describe sport climbing in order to define traditional climbing. A style or methodology doesn't receive the label "traditional" unless it is the earlier standard, and a new and different trend (in this case, sport climbing) arises to define it as such. Comparisons help you differentiate the two styles.

Traditional Lead Climbing relies on a linear approach to learning that emphasizes slow and steady progress with the guidance of a mentor or experienced trad climber. Chapters 1 and 2 explain where traditional leading fits into the realm of roped rock climbing as a whole, and details the psycho-social joys and challenges involved. After reading these chapters, you might ask yourself, *Do I have what it takes?* Chapter 3 describes the hardware and tools you'll need, and Chapters 4 and 5 emphasize technical skill building in low-risk environments.

Chapters 6 and 7 are devoted to more advanced trad lead skills, including multipitch techniques, and an introduction to the fundamentals of self-rescue. Chapter 8 provides information on knot and rope craft, while discussions of ratings, climbing etiquette, and impact and access issues are found in Chapter 9. Following the main text is an appendix, as well as a glossary where I define common climbing vernacular. Throughout the book, each time a technical term or jargon is introduced, it appears in **bold italics** and is defined in the Glossary.

Some of the most valuable information in *Traditional Lead Climbing* stems from the gleanings of several of America's most talented traditional leaders, presented throughout the book in the form of advice and tales of their own learning. These contributors shed light on numerous facets of traditional leading, from partnerships to more technical information on placing gear, falling, and retreating.

The information presented in this book is not intended to be used as a set of protocols you can fall back on at every turn. Trad climbers are most successful when they alternate between protocol and judgment-based decisions. In your beginning years, it's certainly wise to lean heavily toward protocol. But with more experience, your judgment and intuition will mature, giving you the ability to make wise and thoughtful assessments of each situation without relying as heavily on protocol. Book-smart novices expect to be safe on the rocks if, at every turn, they simply do what the protocol suggests. Although probably intelligent and talented, these folks are often some of the most dangerous climbers out there: they never allow their judgment and intuition to blossom. Eventually they run into a problem they don't ever recall reading about. Though ready to initiate a canned solution, they are stumped when the solution requires logic and a combination of skills they possess.

To those learning the craft of traditional lead climbing, keep in mind that most of us are out there pursuing these techniques because we want to have fun. Don't take yourself too seriously, laugh a lot, be safe, and enjoy the ride.

Chapter 1

Rock Climbing 101

What is traditional ("trad") climbing, and what is its relationship to sport climbing? To free climbing? To aid climbing? Where does leading and top-roping fit into the picture? Aspiring rock climbers currently entering the sport frequently ask these questions. For answers, you can begin by examining roles within the typical climbing partnership, as well as by studying fundamental ascent systems and methods. But the paradigm doesn't really come into focus without some sort of historical context. By exploring the recent evolution of the roped rock-climbing experience, you gain a general understanding of the most common techniques and styles used today.

Dave Nettle Collection

ROLES & SYSTEMS

Leading is a roped ascent system with two people fulfilling roles as *leader* and *belayer* and, sometimes, *follower*. In another system known as *top-roping*, the partnership involves a climber and belayer.

Top-Roping

If you are the belayed climber in this system, a rope redirected through an *anchor* above protects you from a serious fall. While your anchored belayer might be situated above you if you are following a route, the belayer is more commonly below you via a *yo-yo* or "slingshot" arrangement. *(Photos: 1-3, opposite page, top)*

Establish an anchor atop a climb—usually no longer than half the distance of your rope—for the yo-yo top-rope. You can either lead the route to establish the anchor, or access the summit via hiking or scrambling.

The belayer of a yo-yo arrangement is situated at the base of the route, and threads a **bight** (or fold) of the rope through his or her **belay device**. The rope runs up through the anchor, and back down to the climber who ties into the other end. The top-rope belayer takes in slack rope as the climber ascends. If the climber falls, the belayer engages the device's braking mechanism and, if properly belayed, the climber falls only the distance that the rope stretches.

Leading *(Photos: 1-3, opposite page, bottom)*

Leading provides the answer to the age-old non-climber question "How do they get their ropes up there?" The belayer pays out rope through a belay device at the bottom of the climb as the leader, tied to one end of the rope, moves up the rock. The leader clips the rope into preestablished **bolts**, or places pieces of **protection** in **cracks** and crevices en route to the **belay stance**, where anchors are either preexisting or created on the spot with the leader's remaining gear.

If the leader falls "on lead," the belayer engages the braking mechanism, so that the rope is halted at the last piece of protection placed. If the piece is secure, the length of the fall will equal the distance above the last piece of protection placed, multiplied by two, plus rope stretch. For instance, if a fall occurs 7' above the leader's last piece, the approximate length of the fall is 14', plus several inches of rope stretch. *(Illustrations: 1-3, pages 10 and 11)*

Once the leader is anchored at the top of the climb, the partners' roles change. Shifting into belayer mode, the leader provides a top-rope for his or her partner, who then takes on the role of **second** (follower) *(Photo: left)*. The second is responsible for **cleaning** (removing) lead gear. Another option if route criteria allows is for the leader to lower from the anchor, cleaning the route as he

Heidi Pesterfield

The second (follower) in action

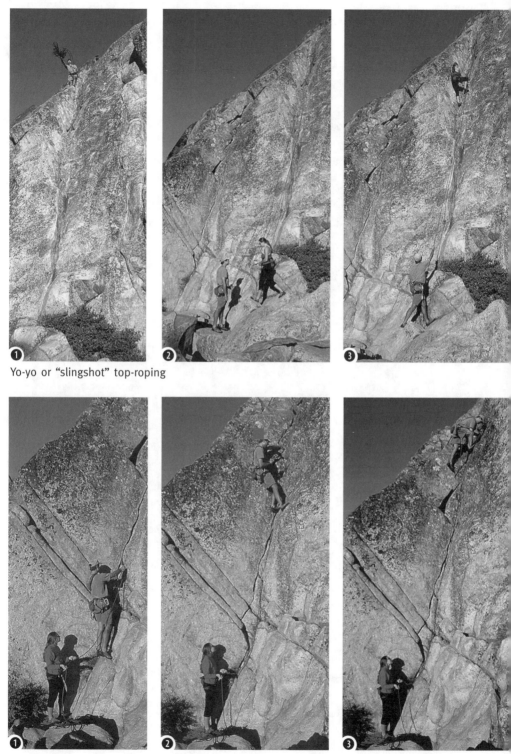

Yo-yo or "slingshot" top-roping

Leading

A typical lead fall

or she descends, thereby establishing a yo-yo top-rope.

BASIC ASCENT METHODS

Free Climbing

Free climbing is often confused with *free soloing*, the act of climbing without a rope and protection. However, free climbing involves roped climbers who wear harnesses and utilize belay systems and climbing hardware for safety.

Free climbing can occur either on lead or top-rope. Traditionally, free climbing means that you attempt to ascend a route by relying upon your own strength, using hand- and footholds for purchase. The rope, protection points, and anchors are only utilized as backups, arresting your fall should a mistake occur. But there are modern ascent tactics in which free climbers use equipment for periodic rests between a series of moves (see "Sport Climbing" and Appendix 2).

Most free climbing today involves *clean lead ascents*, meaning without the use of *pitons* (pins) as protection. From the turn of the 20th Century through the mid-1960s, pitons were carried up free routes and hammered into cracks for lead protection. But during the early '70s, preservation issues related to the increasing rock damage by hammering fueled what is known as the "clean climbing revolution" (see Appendix 1). The elimination of pitons on free climbs was eventually supported by the mass production of alternate, lightweight hardware that could be placed into cracks and removed with relative ease, all without the need for a hammer. I discuss these devices along with other equipment in Chapter 3.

Pitons are still used occasionally on free routes, particularly on first ascents when leaders lack opportunities to place low-impact hardware. In such cases, a piton is often chosen over the more time-consuming and expensive option of placing a bolt.

Direct-Aid Climbing

Direct-aid (aka *artificial climbing*, *illustration: left*) is another method of ascent. Aid techniques provide options when the wall is too steep or blank to allow passage via free climbing. In this method you physically weight each piece of protection, ascending upward via paired webbing ladders called *étriers* (aiders). Used in *big wall* climbing, aid climbing is sometimes alternated with free climbing on such routes.

The ascent of the second in aid climbing is supported by the use of mechanical *ascenders*, known generically as *Jumars*. These devices slide up the rope, but not down. Piton craft is still common on some big walls. Clean-aid ascents are also popular, providing significant challenges for climbers up for the task. Severely scarred piton cracks are notoriously difficult to protect with clean-climbing gear.

Alpine Climbing

Alpine climbing (aka *mountaineering*) involves climbing on varied terrain in a mountain setting. Snow and/or ice and rock are all a part of the alpine game. Many alpine routes involve a combination of free climbing and aid climbing, while others are strictly free. The free climbing style employed in alpine climbing is "traditional" in origin (see "Traditional Free Climbing" below). An alpine route exclusively involving ice is referred to as *ice climbing*, which utilizes its own distinct tools and methods of ascent.

FREE CLIMBING STYLES

The development of new and diverse styles has marked 20th Century climbing. In *Basic Rockcraft* Royal Robbins defines a "style" as the sum of methods and equipment used, plus the degree of adventure involved in the ascent. The emergence of a new climbing style often followed technological advances that allowed climbers to accomplish more difficult routes, usually with increased safety.

The development of tools as complex as the nylon rope and the *spring-loaded camming device (SLCD)*, and

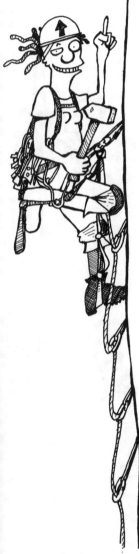

Direct-aid climbing

as simple as the *hip belay* and sticky rubber have all ush-
ered in tremendous changes. But no development has
resulted in changes more momentous than that of the
drill and expansion bolt. Several decades after their
introduction, the drill and expansion bolt gave rise to the
two, distinctive free climbing styles dominant at crags
today—*traditional free climbing* and *sport climbing*.

Existing under the free climbing umbrella, traditional free and sport climbing employ similar principles
of ascent and roles, but vastly different techniques, tools,
and skills. *(Illustrations: 1 and 2 following page).* Prior to
the development of sport climbing in the 1980s, "traditional" rock climbing remained virtually undefined. As
sport climbing's popularity increased worldwide,
descriptive labels became necessary to distinguish the
styles. Labels like "adventure climbing," "classic climbing," and "gear-leading" were frequently used to
describe trad ascents, while "modern free climbing" was
used occasionally to describe sport climbing. Today the
terms "traditional" and "sport" are well anchored in the
climbing vernacular.

Traditional Free Climbing

In his June 1999 article in *Climbing* No. 186, writer
Jeff Achey describes the concept of traditional climbing
with disarming frankness: "Bolts and hardware don't
grow naturally on cliffs. One of the defining characteris-
tics of trad climbing is that you climb raw rock, and protect your own ass."[1] Traditional free climbing involves
ascending a route from the *ground up*, spontaneously
placing pieces of removable protection from the *rack*
wherever you deem necessary or as the rock yields. A
traditional rack varies depending on the route and the
climbing area. It is generally composed of an assortment
of standard clean-climbing hardware of varying sizes
and brands in combination with *runners* (aka *slings*),
quickdraws, and *carabiners*. The trad climbing rack is
discussed at length in Chapter 3.

Though numerous elements are involved in a mas-
terful trad lead, placement of secure and solid protection
while maintaining mental and physical composure tops
the list. Hemingway's description of courage as "grace
under pressure" best portrays the successful trad leader,

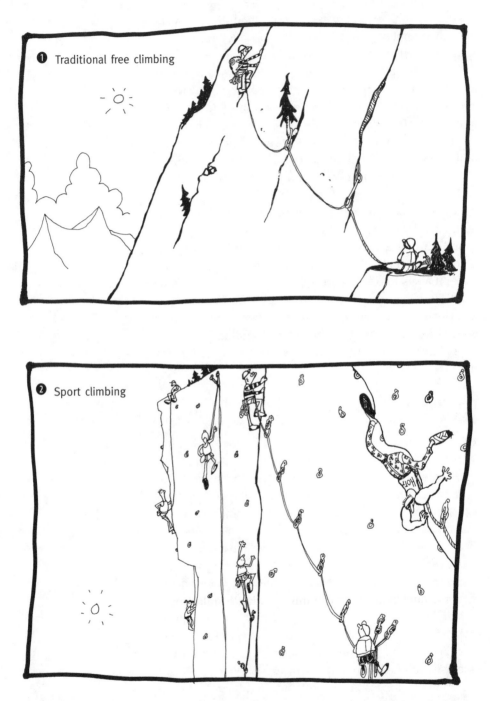

Examples of traditional free and sport climbing that employ similar principles of ascent and roles, but vastly different techniques, tools, and skills.

who balances the physical demands of climbing with the mental tasks of deciding where and how to place gear. The complexity of placing solid protection involves several factors: knowing when to stop and place a piece; knowing how to rest efficiently; deciding how to creatively use what's available on the rock and from your rack; understanding the mechanics of each piece of protection; and evaluating gear size, fit, and rock quality. All these factors play a role in the integrity of each lead.

Traditional routes commonly but not always follow *crack systems*. Climbers on traditional routes frequently encounter *faces* protected by tied-off knobs, slung horns and flora, or bolts placed on lead (hence the term "ground up"). Most trad climbs involve some of each, depending on the morphology of the rock.

Trad climbs vary in length, and are measured in terms of pitches. A *pitch* is the distance between belay stances (anchors), and generally does not exceed the length of the rope. Trad routes can be a single pitch, or a combination of several. Except when a yo-yo system is established on certain single-pitch routes, a partner is required to follow a trad lead to clean protection. If the route continues for more than one pitch, partners will generally swap gear and roles at the top of each. The second now becomes the leader, and the leader becomes the follower. This is the *multipitch* concept, discussed at length in Chapter 6.

Trad climbs are determined by the natural existing features of the rock; therefore, some routes may involve climbing sections that are either difficult or impossible to protect. Such sections are called *runouts*. For instance, the security of a hand-sized crack may peter out into an insidious difficult-to-protect groove. Or the pimply features on a knobby face can diminish gradually, taking on the peaches-and-cream complexion of a smooth wall that will not accept protection. Although many traditional routes offer ample opportunity for protection, most trad leaders accept the fact that runouts are often a part of the game.

Though belay anchors on traditional routes are sometimes preestablished with *fixed gear* such as bolts and pitons, most routes require establishing removable protection. The traditional leader is constantly in gear-conservation mode to leave enough equipment for adequately protecting the rest of the climb and creating a safe belay anchor. The anchor (aka the *belay*) is located at the end of each pitch.

Communication can be difficult on traditional routes. As the leader, you often climb out of your belayer's sight and range of hearing. Your belayer's visual clue to your progress is sometimes limited to the inch-by-inch movement of the rope slithering up and across the rock face, disappearing around a corner or over a bulge.

Sport Climbing

Sport climbs occur on generously bolted routes that are usually established by *rap-bolting*, using power drills while *rappelling* from the top. Yet some sport routes are established "on lead," usually with the assistance of direct-aid. Sport climbs are almost always protected exclusively by bolts, although some might require the placement of a piece of gear or two. Most involve steep-face climbing on vertical-to-overhanging surfaces.

The abundance of closely placed bolts on sport routes eliminates much of the danger that you face in traditional routes, where placing protection is critical, complex, and time-consuming. Because this responsibility is lifted when leading a sport route, you can focus on continuity and difficulty; you can push your physical and mental limits and risk relatively safe, short falls.

A standard sport rack typically consists of several quickdraws assembled with specialized lightweight carabiners for clipping bolts and anchors. The equipment theme in sport climbing is "go light."

Most sport routes require less than half the length of a standard rope, providing leaders the option of a relatively easy retreat, by having the belayer lower them from any bolt. Using less than half the rope length also offers them the opportunity, after reaching the top, to descend via lowering, establishing a yo-yo top-rope to protect subsequent climbers. Typically, the sport belayer is situated directly below the leader, and close enough for relaxed casual communication.

Sport climbs are often rehearsed at length. The leader "works" a route that he or she was previously unable to climb without falling or hanging on the rope. Working a route entails requesting frequent tension from your belayer so you can rest (hang) between difficult sections. Your eventual goal is to climb the route in one push from bottom to top with no falls or hangs. Known as the *red-point*, this mastery can take hours, days, or even months to achieve. Other styles of working routes, some of which are employed on traditional as well as on sport routes, are discussed in Appendix 2.

Although the dangerous elements of traditional free climbing dwarf those of sport climbing, leading sport routes can still be hazardous. Improperly *back-clipping* bolts can result in the disconnection of the rope from carabiners on quickdraws, and erroneous rope positioning can flip the leader upside down if a fall occurs, making head injuries likely without a helmet. Bolts can be *manky* (old and deteriorating), compromising their strength and security. In addition, some first-ascent parties fail to space bolts close enough to protect the leader safely at all points on the route, resulting in the rare but occasional runout sport route.

GROWING PAINS

Recent Changes

Like other changes in climbing history, the emergence in the 1980s of sport climbing did not occur overnight. Trends that laid the groundwork for this new method were in the works years before, mostly in Europe but also on a more covert level in the US (see Appendix 3).

Once sport climbing caught on, conspicuous changes occurred rapidly within the sport, as well as in the climbing industry. First, the continuous-move difficulty ceiling was broken as talented, visionary sport pioneers utilized new tactics to establish routes previously considered unclimable. New bolted-climbing areas developed seemingly overnight, and ratings everywhere shot skyward. Then, a plethora of specialized gear and apparel erupted on the outdoor retail market to arm and outfit sport climbers. Of course, the indoor-climbing concept spread like wildfire, inspiring mainstream interest and an eventual dissolution of climbing's former dare-devil reputation. Eventually, these changes helped to launch the sport of climbing into the largest popularity explosion in its history.

Resistance & Ethical Debates

Changes within the sport were initially met with heated debates by two predominant factions whose voices have accompanied almost every new development in the sport for the past 100 years. The first group was made up of climbers who wholeheartedly embraced new technologies and methods as a way to push the sport's standards and complete more difficult routes. The second included those who consider themselves purists and seek aesthetics in a "less-is-more" adventure. For some of these climbers, the less reliance on technology, the more valuable the experience. Some free climbers of this faction suggest that if climbers can't succeed on a route without bringing the difficulty level down to their ability, perhaps they should climb something easier.

A fierce volleying of ethical accusations and criticism ensued for several years over establishing routes on rappel specifically, and sport-climbing tactics in general. Traditionalists were paranoid that the rap-bolters' enthusiasm might transform their favorite walls into a grid of bolts, attracting swarms of people to otherwise quiet and serene crags. Sport aficionados complained that traditionalist dinosaurs, clinging to outdated methods, prevented the sport from moving forward. Trad climbers accused sport climbers of diminishing the value of achievement within the sport; sport pioneers and their young, talented protégés defended new tactics by thumbing their noses at old-schoolers with every new 5.13 they established. These heated debates were fueled by extreme emotions, probably comparable to the notorious debates in Yosemite Valley regarding the reliance on bolts and the use of fixed ropes on big walls in the 1960s (see Appendix 4).

Around 1988 I recall feeling the pressure to choose one style or the other. But with time tempers softened and the general tenor of these debates changed. Both factions slowly came to embrace the "to each his own" aphorism, probably realizing that the choices climbers were making had less to do with ethics than with style. As a result, rap-bolted routes and sport-climbing tactics slowly became more and more accepted. Today most climbers tolerate and perhaps even enjoy both styles of free climbing.

Rock Climbing Today

Since the advent of sport climbing, the popularity of all facets of rock climbing has skyrocketed. According to a recent study conducted by the Outdoor Industry Association (OIA, formerly called the Outdoor Recreation Coalition of America) with Leisure Trends and the Gallup organization, in 1998, 1.1 million people in the US were climbing enthusiasts (those owning a harness and rope who went climbing over six times that year). Although this figure saw a slight decrease in 1999, the number of participants (people who went climbing at least once during the year) increased from 5.1 to 5.7 million. While there are virtually no scientific studies conducted prior to these dates for comparison, longtime climbers know that these figures reflect a tremendous increase.

Now that you have a clear picture of what modern roped rock climbing looks like today, take a closer look at traditional lead climbing—its unique joys and challenges. In delving into the psyche of the traditional leader, Chapter 2 examines trad leading's relationship to adventure, psychology, and personal ambition.

Heidi Pesterfield

Chapter 2

Exploring the Traditional Lead Experience

A CLOSER LOOK

Traditional climbing is a complex and demanding endeavor spurring adventure, camaraderie, creativity, intuition, spontaneity, and commitment. It challenges you to be honest about your limitations, and entices you by providing access to extraordinary places. It can be an extremely rewarding and joyous experience, or it can be a hair-raising joyride. It is always dangerous. Jeff Achey has neatly summarized the experience:

> Key to the feeling [of traditional climbing] is invoking the spirit of mountain and crag, the inherent hazards and joys. As a trad climber you can't be squeamish. You'll be up on cliffs when it rains. You'll use loose handholds. On a great day maybe you'll get lost, cold, scared, and hungry. And when you make it back, a can of beans never tasted so good, and the campfire feels like the warm embrace of Mother Earth herself.[2]

Adventure

It's obvious that the risks of trad leading far out-weigh those of the sport lead. Why take added risks? Adventure. The adventure of gear-leading frees the climber in you. On sport turf you connect the dots up a line of pre-placed bolts with few surprises. In what is essentially a gymnastic exercise, you can see every bolt—even the anchors at the top. You know exactly how many quickdraws to bring. You know that your partner will lower you to the ground when you're ready—whether it be at the anchors or when you're simply too spent to make the next move.

Yet when you set off on a gear-lead, you open the door to the unknown. From the ground, you may not be able to see the entire pitch. You may not know if an established anchor awaits you at the top, or whether you'll need to conserve gear to build your own. Your bringing the right gear depends on how well you read the rock from the ground. You'll rely on your topo map, as well as your own navigational skills and intuition to find your way upward. As you ascend, the route unfolds unexpectedly, one move at a time. Each corner turned or bulge surmounted offers its challenge.

Commitment

The risk-taking inherent in trad leading keeps commitment levels high. On a sport lead, if you're climbing poorly or the weather takes a turn for the worse, you can almost always retreat with ease. This is rarely so when you lead a trad route. While you may be able to retreat by lowering back down to the belay, you can't depend upon it. Often there aren't solid gear options left when you run out of steam. Sometimes the route traverses so much that lowering wouldn't put you anywhere near your belayer. Most commonly you've used more than half the rope and a quick descent to the belay isn't an option. A trad lead commitment to both the summit and your partner must be bona fide. You are always climbing at your best, because if you aren't your life may be at risk.

Creativity

The craft of the traditional lead is enticing because it provides vast opportunities for individual expression and creativity. Every gear-lead is itself a unique creation—a masterpiece, if you will. Free to place the pieces that you want, where you want, and when, you can stand or rest here, or there. You can place a piece here if you're short, or up there if you're taller. You can muscle your way up the flake because you're better at cracks, or tiptoe around it onto the face because you're slab-happy. You can jam the crack straight on or lie it back. You can place two pieces because the move ahead looks difficult or the landing dangerous, or forgo protection for a ways when the terrain is less challenging and speed essential.

When protection is difficult or sparse, a little creativity accomplishes a lot. When with few resources you're challenged with complex situations, you require the leader's ingenuity to improvise solutions. Though as a beginning trad leader your bag of tricks is minimal, as your experience increases your bag fills, resulting in the ability to cope with increasingly complex situations with just a handful of tools.

Multidimensionality

The traditional gear-lead has numerous facets. With a number of priorities constantly jockeying for your attention as leader, your focus shifts rapidly between climbing movement, placing protection, and route finding. Each requires a degree of technical and physical prowess impossible without remaining calm and focused. Add to this list weather considerations, rack organization, partner communication, energy and gear conservation, rope positioning, runnering, evaluation of rock quality, and anchoring, and you can understand why many leaders are overwhelmed on their first few trad forays. The challenge lies in working toward careful prioritizing, attempting to remain flexible, and mastering the delicate skill of shifting from one concept to the other and back without sacrificing mindfulness.

Camaraderie

Friendships built within the complex emotional framework of a shared adventure are gifts of traditional climbing. Swapping leads on multipitch routes has fast-forwarded more friendships than I can count. Even an afternoon of climbing single trad pitches can provide the basis of a lifetime friendship, opening the door to a sort of intimacy less common outside the realm of adventure. Here's an analogy: Spending an afternoon sport cragging is like spending an afternoon on a guided tour with an acquaintance on a paved bike path in a city park. A day spent swinging leads on a multipitch trad climb is like sharing a maniacal rickshaw ride down the unpaved backstreets of Katmandu with another traveler, unsure if the driver is sober or knows your destination. As trad-climbing partners, you're vulnerable and exposed to each other. Fear, joy, and trust meld to create an unforgettable experience. This quality of traditional leading makes time shared on the crags extremely precious and sacred, and traditional climbs memorable.

Access

Beyond its adventure the one aspect that trues my heart to traditional climbing is access. Trad leading skills are key in ascending routes in some of the most spectacular environments on the planet. While there are some lovely sport climbing locales, if you fancy the thought of ascending spires, towers, and ridges in wilderness settings, it's likely you access their summits by means of traditional gear routes. By means of logistics long routes on such crags are generally incompatible with sport climbing. In terms of sheer numbers, the vast majority of established rock climbing routes in the world involve gear placement.

PSYCHOLOGICAL FACTORS

The psychological fitness required of the trad leader involves a unique ability to concentrate on the task at hand, shift from one task to another, cope with fear and danger, and honor personal limitations.

Concentration

Concentration is a skill required of all leaders. Traditional leads in particular demand a climber's utmost

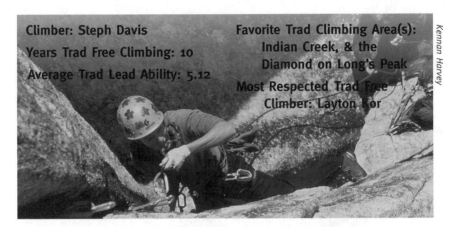

Climber: Steph Davis
Years Trad Free Climbing: 10
Average Trad Lead Ability: 5.12

Favorite Trad Climbing Area(s): Indian Creek, & the Diamond on Long's Peak
Most Respected Trad Free Climber: Layton Kor

Kennan Harvey

Talking Yourself Through Fear & Suffering

To stay mentally focused during hard trad leads, I've had to cope effectively with two common stumbling blocks: fear and suffering. The techniques I use to negotiate both issues involve talking to myself. When I'm most successful negotiating with pain and suffering, I actually hear my voice inside my head—it's that calculated.

Fear—If I'm really afraid, I try to moderate my breathing and concentrate on the nuts and bolts of safety. I run down a mental checklist in my head to make sure the basics are covered. Is my protection the best that it can possibly be? Is the rope positioned properly? Am I using all the best footholds and handholds? Sometimes when you're really scared, you just can't see—it's as if you've become blinded by fear. So if you calm your mind long enough to bring these three basic things into focus, you will reinforce your feeling of being safe, which in turn makes you less afraid.

Suffering—Some climbs—long desert crack climbs spring to mind—are hard because the climbing actually hurts. The pitch may be quite safe but, as it drags on and the physical pain increases, deep down inside you begin to think of giving up—you lose interest in getting to the top. When I'm grinding through something like this, I remember that when it's over I'll be glad I persevered. As a waitress in Moab, my mantra for pushing through on Indian Creek pitches was Would you like some more iced tea? When muscles are screaming, body's hurting, and I'm having a hard time finding motivation to keep going, I remind myself that I'd given up on law school, a Ph.D., and many other opportunities so that I could be doing this, so I damn well better give it my all!

—Steph Davis

attention, because even slight distractions can lead to dire consequences. Obstacles that make focusing difficult generally stem from internal distractions, holding us captive in either the past or the future. Your mind generates distractions that take a variety of forms. On some days, "the committee" discusses whether or not you have the skills to succeed on the chosen route. Other days you mentally rehash the argument you had with a loved one earlier in the day, thinking of all the things you should have said but didn't. And sometimes your mind will avoid the present moment by creating lists—what to buy at the store for dinner, climbing areas you'd like to visit, routes you'd like to climb, jobs for which you'd like apply—and the lists go on.

To lead climb effectively you need ways to screen out distractions. You could explore the finer points of stabilizing the mind through relaxation and breathing techniques. Meditating regularly can also improve concentration skills by enhancing awareness. As you develop the ability to relax on lead, you notice that in the present moment your busy mind stabilizes, your focus increases, and your performance becomes enhanced.

Decision-making & Multitasking

On gear-leads be prepared to make split-second decisions while juggling a multitude of equally important tasks. Your success will stem from confidence and intuition gained from experience and time on the rock. Most decisions you make as the leader will affect the safety of both you and your partner. In the beginning, the multitasking nature of trad leading will overwhelm you. You'll wonder how to ever focus on the physical aspect of climbing itself. For awhile the trad lead will be all about gear and you'll barely remember making moves between pieces. As your skills develop over time, though, your movements take on a natural flow—you're able to focus on the climbing at hand while calmly addressing other tasks as they arise. When decision-making becomes second nature, situations that once were colossal are easily resolved.

Coping with Fear & Danger

For the traditional leader, ineffectively coping with fear threatens safety, let alone success. Yet fear *can* be healthy. By fostering your respect for (and attention to) the mountains and nature, it keeps you alive. But at its worst it's a liability morphing into terror, then panic and, soon, paralysis. To lead trad routes you must manage and channel fear into a useful energy that doesn't undermine your goals.

Climber Marc Twight describes how to use self-discipline to harness fear and transform it into a source of strength:

> To climb through fear, to point fear up instead of down, you need to maintain the desire and strength, the will and discipline, to go until the end of the pitch. If you are scared, reinforce your confidence by biting off what you know you can chew. Successfully swallowing it will encourage you to take another bite, another pitch...Trust in your skill, and give yourself up to the action.[3]

Although Twight addresses extreme alpine climbing, his description of manipulating fear can apply in nearly any climbing scenario. If you are the type of person likely to respond to urgent situations with thoughtful action rather than immobilization, you're probably capable of transforming fear into fuel to keep you safe and moving upward, a little at a time.

AMBITION

By providing the momentum needed to accomplish goals and gain confidence, ambition plays a positive role in your life, whether it be expressed in attending a job interview, giving a presentation at work, or running a marathon. In climbing, ambition lets you progress in skill level by your willingness to tackle increasingly difficult routes. To advance safely in the trad leading sphere, though, your ambition must balance desire with a healthy dose of reason.

Climber: Ron Kauk

Years Free Climbing: 30

Average Trad Lead Ability: Depends on the day

Favorite Trad Climbing Area(s): Earth

Most Respected Trad Free Climber: The Blue Bellied Lizard

Chris Falkenstein

Lead Climbing & Human Development

Leading allows you the opportunity to work in a balanced way with all of the elements of your humanness: emotion, judgment, ability, ego. It's an unbelievable teacher and educator. That's the beauty of bothering yourself to put on a rack and climb up a rock really—all this potential human development. The way you are on lead is a direct reflection of your approach to everyday life. Are you organized? Are you respectful toward the natural world? Are you hurried? Flexible? Humble? Are you trying to prove something to someone else? Egos are very tricky. They can sneak up on you and play games with your mind. Just when you're convinced you are operating without ego is often the time when it's bigger than ever, simply because you believe this. It's nuts! If you become egotistical about your achievements and believe you are superior because you have something more than everyone else, you're in trouble. You miss the point, and any positive aspect of your experience will backfire. You could actually become arrogant enough that your ego will walk you right off the side of a cliff. As a new leader, follow your own experience and avoid comparing yourself to anyone else. Your true strength will shine in your ability to humble yourself and connect with the natural world with balance and respect. We're all equal whether you believe it or not.

—Ron Kauk

Honoring Personal Limitations

Problems develop when the excitement of achieving a climbing goal interferes with a clear appraisal of your capabilities. According to American Alpine Club (AAC) data for the past five years, climbers misjudging their abilities has been one of the most common contributing causes of reported accidents in both the US and Canada.

A difficult task for climbers is to resist the desire of "having done" one route or another. During my first season in Yosemite I found myself so enthralled by the talk of big walls that I committed myself to a route high above the valley floor where I, unskilled and frightened, faced tasks I was completely unprepared for. A route that most climbers at that time completed in a day and a half took my partner and me three days. My overzealous will to have done a big wall, together with my misappraised abilities, endangered us. I became so flustered while attempting to follow a traversing aid pitch that I panicked and froze, requiring that my partner rappel down to help me. After our ropes became a tangled macramé, we spent our last daylight hour disentangling the mess. We discovered at one point to our horror that we had both untied from the rope and clipped off the same, single, fixed piton, circa 1950 no doubt.

A few days later, after miraculously summiting unharmed, we were safely back down on the Valley floor. When an experienced local climber commented that I "had no business going up there," I recall being miffed. Years later I realized this person had been right. Being accepted by my peers for having done a big wall at the time completely overshadowed my awareness that I didn't have adequate experience or skills. A year later I returned to the Valley with many more skills and experience on the rock, and safely completed two additional walls in decent time and with no major *epics*.

Questioning Motives

Thinking your climbing goals through requires rigorous awareness of your motives, as well as your skill level. Had I taken the time to think through my first big wall adventure, I would have recognized I had more work to do before taking on that challenge. I would have recognized my ego working to convince me I could do whatever made me look cool. Veiled by ambition lurk some very dangerous intentions, tilted heavily toward desire but light on reason and humility.

When you find yourself at the base of a challenging route desiring to climb it, because so and so is at the crags and you want to show off, because everyone else you know has led it, or simply because you'd like to tick it off your list, take a minute to adequately assess your abilities. Remember there's a lot more at stake on trad climbs. Are you puffed up with unbalanced ambition? Are you succumbing to peer pressure? A climber who lives to climb another day can walk away from a trad climb and acknowledge *Not today* or *I'm not ready*.

Mike Davis Collection

Chapter 3

Tools of the Trad

Traditional leading requires specific gear. Your previous climbing experience has most likely resulted in the acquisition of a harness, shoes, belay device, *chalk bag*, rope, and a modest rack for top-roping. If you're coming into the trad realm by means of sport climbing, you may have a few more items. Although some crossover use is possible, climbing gear has become so highly specialized that you're probably going to need an entirely new set of tools.

The equipment listed in this chapter is generalized. The gear you ultimately choose must fit the type of rock and routes on which you'll most frequently be leading. Specific gear-placement techniques are discussed in Chapter 4.

Some relish the task of acquiring the necessary accouterments for trad leading—especially those self-styled gearheads or equipment nerds—but nearly everyone balks at the costly investment. If you gear-lead with a trustworthy friend, you can cut your initial costs in half. I'm not recommending sharing gear but rather each climber owning half of the gear to complete a rack. After the initial investment, you can both leisurely fill out your individual racks over time. This way you find out what products you prefer without depleting the pocketbook. But you both still need your own personal harness, shoes, chalk bag, *rappel device*, and *nut tool*.

When it comes to manufacturing climbing gear—particularly hardware—wisdom comes with age. Purchase brands and styles with longevity on the market. Tried and true items have spent a lot of time in research and development labs, as well as in the hands of product testers. If a product has been around for several years, it has gone through several stages of refinement, thereby providing superior performance than some of the newer styles and brands. The latest thing may be no more than that.

To identify your gear, mark hardware and runners with colored electrical tape. Some climbers prefer to etch their initials into hardware—this lasts forever but takes a significant time commitment. Sort gear after every climb to ensure it stays in your possession. I am now a fanatic about sorting, after years of slow but steady gear loss. No one intentionally "adopts" your gear, it just happens when so much is community property.

BASIC EQUIPMENT

Shoes

Find a knowledgeable salesperson with traditional climbing experience to help you choose a shoe for trad routes. Most salespeople offering to help with climbing boots are unqualified to do so, especially in larger chain stores. With such a pricey investment you want to walk out with the right pair. If you can't find an informed sales clerk, bring along someone with trad savvy, or at least first obtain a few style and brand recommendations from someone you trust. Another option might be to borrow or rent a pair of shoes to see how they feel on real rock. This is an optimal solution, though it limits size and brand options.

Since traditional cragging involves varied terrain, an all-round model is often a good starter shoe. Look for a moderately stiff pair you think you'll be able to tolerate wearing all day. Most of these are going to have a substantial midsole to support the foot as your muscles develop. You'll probably want to avoid choosing a pair that has an extremely cambered design (which resembles the arched spine of an angry cat), mainly because it lacks the support and comfort of good beginner trad climbing shoes. Modeled after a foot with down-curled toes, extremely cambered boots are used for high performance sport climbing.

A high-top boot that protects your ankles in cracks is a wise choice, especially if you'll be climbing a lot of cracks that are hand-size and larger. Unfortunately, only a few manufacturers still make high tops. Slippers are ideal for bouldering and on short, thin crack routes, but I don't recommend them as your primary trad-climbing shoe. Not as versatile, they'll be murder on your feet in wider cracks and on long routes, and will wear much faster since they are usually made with significantly less rubber than lace-ups.

Consider purchasing a second, more specialized pair for terrain on which you'll be climbing most. Eventually, you'll want to have at least two pairs of trad shoes on hand anyway—one to take the place of a pair that's blown out and needs repair. Most veteran climbers own several pairs for a variety of venues. Your second pair for trad cragging may be a bit softer—perhaps a pair with a more flexible midsole for increased sensitivity and fancy footwork. Or, if you find yourself frequently on wide cracks and long routes, a more specialized, super stiff boot might serve you well.

Beware of salespeople convincing you to buy a size so tight that your feet scream out in pain. While climbing boots are not designed to be as comfortable as street shoes, the trad fit should be snug, not painful. If your toes curl in the toe box, try a larger shoe. Spend some time in the boots you're considering; take a stroll around the shop a few times. Do some bouldering if the shop has an artificial wall for that purpose.

Although you're looking for comfort, make sure the fit isn't sloppy. If your feet slide around or rotate inside the boots when laced up, they're probably too big. Most climbing shoes stretch a little, but not a lot. Stretch occurs mostly in width, and more with shoes sans lining. Socks are a personal choice. I don't wear them but my boots collect perspiration odor, and I suffer when temperatures drop. If you prefer socks, try a thin, polyester-blend liner sock. The bulkier the sock, the more sensitivity is lost.

Harness

Choose a harness for trad climbing with five important features: padded waist belt, a minimum of two gear loops, one rear *haul loop*, and easily released, padded leg loops. Leg loops that easily unhitch are essential for when nature calls, and are an absolute must for women. They also allow for putting on another clothing layer without unbuckling your harness. Surprisingly, many harnesses available do not offer this feature. Some harnesses on the market also lack a haul loop. However, a short (6" or 2.4cm) sewn runner can be used to modify such a harness with minimal alteration and sewing. In terms of padding, you will definitely appreciate the comfort of wide, significantly padded waist belts and leg loops on long routes, at hanging belays, and on descents that require multiple rappels. While adjustable leg loops are not absolutely necessary, they do allow adjustment for the varied thickness of your clothing. And if you gain or lose a few pounds, you probably won't have to purchase a new harness.

A properly fitting harness will be snug but not tight. If possible, try on the harness you're thinking of purchasing and, literally, hang in it. If the waist belt rides high up on your ribs, or if the leg loops instead of becoming taut tend to dangle loosely below your crotch, try something smaller. The waist belt should have at least a 3" (7.5mm) tail after doubling back.

Belay/Rappel Device

Not counting *figure-eight devices*, there are over 20 *belay plates*, *belay tubes*, and auto-locking devices available on the market today—a far cry from the slim pickings of ten years ago. Because they are versatile, lightweight and technically superior, tubes work best for trad climbing. Shop for a device that best suits the rope diameter you will be using. Figure-eights and plates are also options but have some drawbacks that I'll discuss later.

If you prefer a tube model, choose one with thick metal walls for optimal heat dissipation. Narrow-walled devices heat up to flesh-searing temperatures. Thicker walls

Various tube model belay devices

Belay plate with spring

also diminish the possibility of grooving, which can create undetectable sharp edges inside the tube that can harm your rope. All tube models have keeper-loops to clip into your locking carabiner. A design with a plastic- or rubber-covered metal loop won't heat up, and its rigidity will help prevent the loop from being sucked into the device. Some models offer options for greater or lesser friction, depending on the diameter of rope you're using as well as the kind of rappel you're executing (i.e. less friction on slabs, more on overhanging rappels). Other designs are more suited for smaller-diameter double ropes.

The belay plate has been around for a long time but few retailers keep them in stock. If you want a plate model you may have to special order it. According to one retailer, the superior technology of today's tube designs—particularly their braking quality—has decreased interest in plate models. Nevertheless they remain an option. Belay plates are available with or without a spring. Buying a plate without a spring can be problematic if the device cinches so tightly against your locking carabiner that it becomes difficult to feed or take in rope with ease, especially after the rope is weighted. However, springs may reduce the holding power of the plate itself, and can get tangled with other gear on your harness.

The figure-eight was originally designed for rappelling but can also be used for belaying. The average eight is often heavier than most tube models, and tends to twist the rope. In addition, the figure-eight has several drawbacks as a rappel device. When it's used for rappelling on low-angle terrain, your progress is slow and laborious. Although rare, if the rope flips into a *girth hitch*, a figure-eight can leave you stranded in midair until you remove all your weight from the device to correct its positioning.

If you prefer the figure-eight, thread a *bight* (loop or bend) of the rope through the smaller hole for belaying *(Photos: 1a and 1b, opposite)*. Choose a model approved for belaying. Stick with the traditional setup for rappelling *(Photo: 2, opposite page, bottom)* and carry cord or non-

Figure-eight

Spectra slings to create a friction hitch (see Chapter 7) to help correct the rope should it flip into a girth hitch. And, finally, don't be tempted to belay a leader by passing a bight of the rope through the larger hole and clipping it directly into your locking carabiner. Belayers have dropped fellow lead climbers using this configuration. Even though it affords smoother rope feeding, the friction is dangerously minimal; this method should be used only for advanced belays by experienced climbers in systems involving a lot of friction (i.e. top-roping).

Figure-eight device rigged for belaying

I don't recommend mechanical camming devices like *GriGri* for trad free climbing—besides being complex and risky for beginners, they're heavy and not designed for rappelling. Contrary to their reputation as foolproof, many accidents occur with them. In addition to being easily misthreaded, the cam mechanism may not engage immediately in slow, low-impact falls. If the release mechanism is obstructed or misunderstood, the cams will fail to engage and lock the rope. To lower a climber, you must gradually release the brake mechanism by pulling a lever toward you. By adjusting the angle of the lever you control speed. If it is fully opened, the climber will fall until the belayer lets go, allowing the spring-loaded lever to close. Many accidents have occurred when novices fail to understand this concept. Their natural instinct says *Don't let go!* and so they pull harder.

In addition, because of their auto-locking capabilities, extended use of mechanical belay devices tends to instill a dangerous sense of passivity when you switch to devices that require proactive belaying. Although many professionals maintain that mechanized camming units are still the best bet for beginners, I think they should be considered a more advanced tool for belay-

Figure-eight device rigged for rappelling

Assortment of large locking carabiners

ing. Save your auto-locking devices for belays on long aid routes or working sport climbs, recognize their limitations, and know how to use them correctly.

Locking Carabiners

Your primary carabiner that links you to your partner while belaying and to the rope while rappelling must be a locking carabiner *(locker)*—the bigger, the better. Choose one with a large diameter opening to easily accommodate more knots and slings if needed. A variety of lock styles are available, the most common being the screw gate. These are fine, as long as you are diligent about locking them, and choose a "gate lock" instead of a "nose lock." The latter can become stuck in the gate-locked position. Spring-loaded auto-locking 'biners are also available. I like both styles. If you choose an auto-locker but also have screw gates on your rack, be sure you don't get so used to the mindless auto-lock feature that you neglect closing the other gates manually.

Another locking carabiner is necessary for clipping yourself into anchors. Although it doesn't need to be as big as your primary locker, the larger it is the more versatile. In addition, you'll need a few more medium-sized lockers for self-rescue, as well as one small one for key lead pieces.

Cordelette or Web-o-lette™

The suggested pre-equalization of anchors discussed in detail in Chapter 4 requires either a cordelette or *Web-o-lette*™. A cordelette is made of 18-25′ (6-8m) of 7mm nylon cord (or smaller of high-performance specialty cord) fastened together with a *ring bend* or a *double fisherman's knot*. The Web-o-lette™ is a 10-12′ (250-300cm) length of Spectra webbing with sewn loops on both ends. More durable and lighter than a standard-length cordelette, it is easy to carry and unknot after use. While the cordelette is often difficult to unknot and prepare for carrying, it is slightly more versatile, particularly in the self-rescue techniques described in Chapter 7.

Ropes

Lead-climbing ropes must be dynamic (rather than static): they stretch to absorb shock and dissipate energy generated by a fall. Made from nylon, they have a kern-mantle construction: a tough inner core (kern) that is the main load-bearing portion of the rope, and an outer sheath (mantle) that protects it from abrasion.

Most trad leaders use either a single-rope or double-rope system for leading, with a twin-rope system being less common. Each system has its pros and cons. Throughout this book, I refer predominately to the single-rope system, requiring ropes identified by a circled number "1" on the label at one end.

The standard length of lead ropes for general rock climbing is gradually shifting from 165' (50m) to 200' (60m). Although most pitches (especially in the US) are still 165' or less, I wouldn't recommend a length less than 200', especially if you plan on traveling, as newer routes (both sport and trad) in many other countries frequently surpass 50m.

In general, the larger the diameter of a rope, the stronger and more durable it is. Rarely seen anymore except in recreational settings are the 11mm workhorses used frequently on big walls, where ropes suffer significant abuse from hauling and ascending. A 10mm rope is a good choice for all-round trad purposes, although some climbers use smaller-diameter single ropes for backcountry ascents, or for red-point attempts when weight might be a factor. By going light you sacrifice durability, and may have to retire your rope sooner than with a larger diameter cord.

Though a "dry" rope costs more, I prefer it over a "non-dry" cord for trad climbing, particularly if you climb multipitch mountainous routes or in areas prone to thunderstorms. Dry ropes receive a treatment that helps prevent rainwater absorption. When a rope has absorbed a lot of water, it becomes heavier and less able to cushion a fall. And in very cold conditions, absorbed water can freeze, making the rope weaker and less manageable. While some treatments wear off with use, products can be purchased and applied to rejuvenate it.

Lead ropes are available in solid colors, bicolors, or bipatterns. The latter assist climbers in quickly locating the midpoint of their ropes. This excellent timesaving feature, which costs a bit more, may also increase safety. If you don't have the extra cash, purchase Blue Water's special rope pen (made without damaging chemicals), mark your rope's center, and reapply as necessary.

Each type of lead rope is tested to failure (until it breaks) and assigned a strength rating based on the number of falls it tolerates. The average ranges from seven to nine and, as you might guess, larger diameter ropes tend to tolerate more falls. So, it is crucial for climbers to be diligent about recording each significant leader fall and retire lead ropes accordingly. (See Chapter 5 for more information on ropes and lead falls.)

Besides fall ratings, ropes are also rated for "maximum impact force" and "static elongation." Static elongation refers to the amount a rope stretches during strength testing when weighted by a load of 176 lbs (80 kg). A low rating means the rope won't stretch as much under load, a favorable characteristic for ropes used specifically for rappelling, hauling, and ascending. A higher elongation rating, which means the rope stretches more under load and is more comfortable for a climber, is desirable for leading.

Maximum-impact force is the force transmitted to a climber during a fall. The lower the impact force, the more the rope absorbs energy generated in a fall, transmitting less to the system and the climber. Since gear isn't always optimal in the trad lead setting, a rope rated for lower maximum impact is preferable in some situations but not necessarily required. Because a lower maximum-impact force translates into more rope stretch, the downside may be a longer fall. (More information on rope strength and loads is discussed in Chapter 5.)

Many climbers who lead on a single rope own a second, smaller-diameter rope specifically for use as a *trail line.* This rope is used for descents requiring double-rope rappels, for hauling a pack, or simply as a backup for unplanned retreats. Your trail line can also be utilized as an emergency lead line should your primary rope become damaged. For this reason you'll want a dynamic trail rope on which you'd feel fairly comfortable leading in an emergency. Personally, I'd lead on a single 9mm in an emergency, but I cringe at the thought of taking the *sharp end* on anything smaller. Others feel differently based on the unlikelihood of such an occurrence and are willing to go lighter.

Handle all climbing ropes with care: avoid stepping on them, and keep them clean and out of the dirt. Rope bags are nice for casual cragging, but don't fit easily into a pack. I carry a square yard of inexpensive nylon tarp material to keep my rope out of the dirt. Immediately retire ropes with damaged sheaths or exposed cores. Exposure to excessive heat (above 120°F or 50°C), sunlight (UV), solvents, or chemicals including uric acid (urine) should also dictate retirement. Other signs of excessive wear that indicate the need for replacement include inconsistency in texture, unusual stiffness or softness, and glossy marks on the sheath. Wash your rope in a bathtub with warm water and no soap. Allow it to dry uncoiled in a warm, dry location out of the sun. Never put your rope in a dryer.

The Sterling Rope Company recommends these general guidelines for rope retirement based on use periods:

• Three months to one year when used frequently and intensively

• About two years when used regularly on weekends

• About two to four years when used occasionally

Helmet

As Russ Walling of FISH Products says, "Helmets are cool." "Brain buckets" have been available for years but the majority of climbers couldn't be bothered—they were uncomfortable, heavy, claustrophobic, and hindered your sight. To top it off, they also looked geeky. Years ago a partner of mine demanded to know in frustration as her helmet slumped over her eyes, "When are the bike helmet people going to get together with the climbing helmet makers?"

Sometime in the mid-'90s climbers began to care more about their noggins than fashion and comfort, and helmets began to sell like gangbusters. In response, manufacturers began funneling more energy into helmet design, resulting in several lightweight models—which are honestly quite comfortable—featuring high-tech ventilation and adjustment systems. Choosing a helmet is simple—find an adjustable, *CEN-* and/or *UIAA*-approved model that best fits your head. Don't order a helmet from a catalog unless you've tried it on and are certain you like the design. Don't end up with a helmet you hate—too easily left at the base of a climb if it even leaves home.

Make sure your helmet adjusts properly for a snug fit. One gear supplier told me his company performed its own tests on helmets and discovered that some, although UIAA-approved, fit poorly after all the manufacturer's directions were followed. If, after adjustments, your helmet shifts even slightly to the back or side of your head, it's not going to provide the proper protection. Be cautious, too, of the super lightweight models; you may want more protection than some of these offer.

A helmet protects you from more than just rockfall. The most common climbing head injuries occur as the result of lead climbing falls. Consider that a falling carabiner, or a shard of ice rocketing down the face of a climb on a warm spring day, can crack a skull, as well. But, since a helmet cannot protect you from extreme impact forces, do what you can to stay out of harm's way (see Chapter 6).

Chalk Bag

You can choose a chalk bag with a color and material design that best suits your personality but, more importantly, find a model on the larger side. Smaller bags are generally designed with sport climbers in mind, who rarely need to chalk up more than their finger tips. Because trad climbers need to coat their entire hands, widemouthed bags make it easy. Misty Mountain Threadworks makes a good large bag, but my favorite design by Black Diamond features a nifty zippered pocket where you can carry an energy bar, topo, keys—whatever.

Nut Tool

Gear-leading requires that the follower carry a nut tool to extract snug nut placements (and sometimes cams) while cleaning each pitch. I always carry my own rather than sharing it with a partner. Many suitable designs are available. Buy one with a hooked tip for removing stuck cams and larger nuts with eyeholes (see Chapter 4). DMM's model with its rubber-clad handle is gentle on my hands and fingers when I get aggro removing a particularly stubborn placement. Your nut tool should be kept on its own carabiner and attached with about 1' (30cm) of small-diameter accessory cord. The tool can then be clipped short for carrying or extended for use *(Photos: 1 and 2).*

Gear Sling

Your *gear sling* should be padded and adjustable. Some companies offer fleece-lined comfort, while others make closed-cell-foam slings. Since trad parties need only one rack at a time, you frequently share your rack with a partner, who may not be your size. Before adjustable gear slings I schlepped my way up routes with gear dangling halfway to my knees, like a kid playing dress-up in adult clothes. I finished each climb with the blackest and bluest thighs seen outside of a shelter. Other women and smaller-framed men can attest to the misery experienced prior to adjustable gear slings.

One particular type of gear sling on the market today features sectioned loops. Unlike most others, the Mountain Speed Sling by Mountain Tools is strong enough to use as as a runner in a pinch. Though I've never used a sectioned gear sling, many climbers like them. Still, a petite friend told me that this style didn't work well on her small frame.

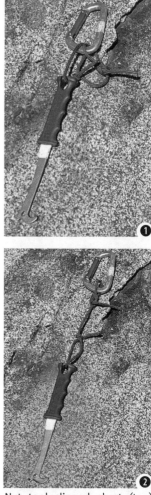

THE RACK

SLCDs (Spring-Loaded Camming Devices)

Nut tool clipped short (top) and extended (bottom)

The invention of the SLCD in the mid-1970s revolutionized gear-leading like no other hardware breakthrough. Cams offer protection where nothing else fits, are easy and fast to place once you learn how, and, if placed correctly, are simple to remove.

With a plethora of SLCDs from which to choose on the market today, most are versatile enough for general use, while some excel for specific applications. Specialty off-set devices work wonders in thin, corrugated cracks and flares but teeter helplessly in parallel-sided *splitters*. A fat, 4-cam

Assorted SLCDs

device offering 35% more surface contact than like-sized cams perfectly addresses desert sandstone climbers' needs, but *try* to get this piece to work in a granite pin scar.

With so many choices available, you may be tempted to own a few of each. For a starter rack, though, stick with just a few brands. Why? Because cam manufacturers, curiously, don't share the same sizing scale, owning various brands means constantly translating from one size range to another. A fairly uniform cam rack in the beginning of your trad career gets you comfortable with a few designs' sizing ranges, color codes, and technical capabilities. If you mix and match brands, your cams won't hang uniformly, making it more difficult while leading to view the cams at a glance. (For a comprehensive comparison chart of SLCDs, see "The Mother of All Cam Charts" in *Rock & Ice* No. 109.)[4] Although a bit outdated, it remains a handy resource. In addition, many mail order companies like Mountain Gear print helpful charts.

SLCD manufacturers offer two stem designs: the U-stem and the central cable. Stem designs probably won't mean much to you as a new trad leader. After some tinkering on lead, however, you may develop a preference. Some stems are more flexible, while others are longer. Triggers vary, too, a detail that is mostly a personal preference depending primarily on hand size. Since operating triggers on some SLCDs may be awkward if you have large hands, spend some in-store time pulling those of various brands before you buy. Or, better yet, borrow an assortment from friends and try them out at your local crags.

For the smaller SLCDs you have the option of either 3- or 4-cam designs. Three-cam units have narrow heads that fit where nothing else will. They are ideal in rounded pin scars and shallow pods. Four-cam units are usually more stable (less likely to pivot) and some possess superior holding power than 3-cam units, but are not as versatile. I prefer a combination because 3-cam SLCDs work wonders at most of the crags I frequent. Talk to local climbers to determine your need for 3-cam units.

The dual-axle design, currently offered only by Black Diamond, offers the greatest expansion range of all SLCDs. The drawback of these beauties is that they are 25-50 percent heavier than similar-sized cams. (And they *are* more expensive.) Yet the flexibility gained from having wider expansion is worth the extra weight and money for new leaders.

A standard SLCD rack adequate for most trad climbing areas has two cams of each size up to approximately 3", and one for sizes 3-4.5". Because this optimal rack makes for an enormous initial investment, you might consider purchasing your 1.5-3" sizes first, and fill in the remaining gaps with less expensive *Stoppers*™ (nuts), Hexes, and Tri-Cams.

A final word on cam purchase: SLCD manufacturers who have been making cams for a long time (like Wild Country, Black Diamond, Colorado Custom Hardware, and Metolius) have an edge over those newer to the game. While other brands can be as good, you have to carefully weigh these purchases when you're hemorrhaging money for gear you hope will last you decades.

Stoppers

Stoppers (aka nuts, *tapers*, or *chocks*) are considered "passive" gear because they have no moving parts. For your trad rack, start with a combination of curved and straight Stoppers. Though curved nuts aren't any stronger than straights, they tend to set better, wrapping around tiny inconsistencies inside the crack. For general terrain, carry doubles of small and medium sizes (¼-¾" or 6-21mm) and singles of micro and larger sizes.

Before purchasing nuts under ¼" (6mm), consider the type of rock on which you'll most often be climbing. If you lead on granite, the superior metal choice for micro nuts is steel or a steel blend. Steel won't deform under stress, while softer metals can shear out of a granite crack. If you're leading on softer rock such as limestone, use brass, bronze, or copper-infused Stoppers because force generated onto a steel nut placement in soft rock can shatter the rock around it.

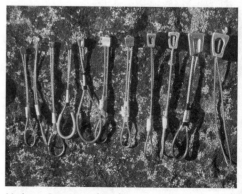
Various Stoppers (nuts)

Offset nuts made by companies like DMM and Hugh Banner (HB) are great specialty pieces that you may choose eventually to add to your standard wired selection. These asymmetrical gems are designed to lock into the rock's subtle irregularities, and work great if you're dealing with sections of corrugated, bottlenecked cracks that aren't parallel.

Hexcentrics & Tri-Cams

Tri-Cams (*Photo: 1*) and **Hexcentrics** (Hexes) (*Photo: 2*) are known as "passive" camming devices and are lighter and far less expensive than SLCDs. Smaller Tri-Cams work particularly well in shallow flares and pin scars. The latest Black Diamond Hex design fits into four different crack configurations, and works best in tapered slots, and Metolius makes a curved design. Drawbacks of these devices are that they take time, patience, and thought to place correctly, and are much less versatile than SLCDs.

Big Bros

Big Bros are pieces of protection for *off-widths* that are generally owned by the more advanced leader, so they're not covered in detail here. A Big Bro is an expandable tube that is screwed into place but also has camming properties. Along with large specialty cams, they have made it possible for today's climbers to safely lead some of the wide and cavernous *testpieces*, previously led with little protection by the bold free climbers of the 1970s.

Carabiners

Consider strength and versatility when choosing carabiners for your trad rack. A combination of standard and asymetrically shaped Ds (*Photo: 3*) is a good choice for most of your 'biner collection. A few ovals (*Photo: 4, opposite page, top*) come in handy for racking **Stoppers**™, performing **carabiner brake rappels** (see Chapter 8), and accommodating multiple knots or webbing. Yet ovals are not as strong as standard Ds. Asymmetrical Ds generally have larger gate openings than standard Ds so clipping is easier. Smaller at one end than the other, they also tend

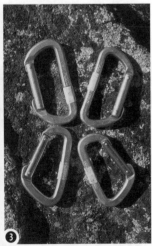

❶
Lowe Tri-Cams

❷
Hexcentrics

❸
Standard (above) and asymetrical (below) "D" carabiners

to be somewhat lighter. However, they aren't as versatile as your standard D.

A carabiner is strongest along its vertical axis. A D-shaped 'biner is stronger than an oval because its shape shifts the load close to the spine and away from its weakest point, the gate. Carabiners have closed- and open-gate strength ratings because gates sometimes open unexpectedly (see Chapter 4). The average strength rating of a 'biner with its gate closed is almost three times that of the same one open.

Bent-gate and wire-gate carabiners *(Photo: 5)* are not as versatile as others but frequently make their way onto trad climbers' racks. The wire-gate 'biner has a very high strength-to weight ratio and boasts an unsurpassed gate opening for its size. Bent gates are easy to clip with one hand from a precarious position when leading, and unclip just as easily. They are used widely in sport climbing. Bent gates are designed specifically for clipping into the rope while climbing, so their use is limited to being the component of a quickdraw or an SLCD sling. Because they lack versatility, I don't carry many on my trad rack. Also, the smaller diameter of some extremely light bent-gate models significantly reduces the strength of the rope: running the rope over a carabiner with a diameter of 10mm or less will reduce its strength by 30 percent or greater.

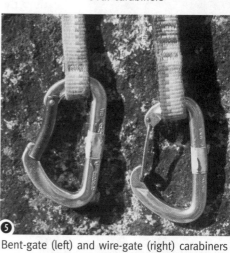

Oval carabiners

Bent-gate (left) and wire-gate (right) carabiners

How many total carabiners will you need? Aside from a 'biner for each SLCD and a couple on which to rack your Stoppers, consider purchasing 20-25 "single" (or free) carabiners for your starter rack. If the pitches are longer in your home cragging area, or if you're going to pursue multipitch routes in which simultaneous belays eat up more of your single carabiners, purchase a few more.

Slings & Quickdraws

Slings (runners) can be purchased pre-sewn or tied at home from nylon webbing bought in bulk. I recommend carrying some of each *(Photo: 6)*. While you can make a longer sling shorter by doubling or

Quickdraws (left) and tied and sewn runners (right)

tripling it, making a short sling longer requires a magic that's beyond me. So, trad leaders benefit from carrying a number of 22-24" (50-60cm) shoulder-length slings, which can either be tripled and carried as quickdraws, or carried full-length over the shoulder.

To make a tripled quickdraw *(Photos: 1-3, opposite)* out of a shoulder-length runner, begin with a runner with a carabiner at each end. Grasp the lower 'biner and bring it up through the top carabiner. Carefully thread a third of the sling through this upper carabiner, and back down to join the other two loops. Now gather the two loops together and secure them with the bottom carabiner. When you need a quickdraw twice that length, unclip one of the loops and extend. Unclip two loops and extend them when you need a full-length sling.

Trad leaders might also consider having a few 48" (120cm) slings. To make this sling more compact for carrying *(Photos: 1-5, page 48)*, begin by doubling it. Next, while holding the doubled sling taut by grasping each end with an index finger, begin twisting both ends simultaneously in opposite directions. After three or four complete twists, join both ends (all four strands) together with a single 'biner, allowing all the strands to spiral around.

Material and width choices for sewn runners include ⁹⁄₁₆-¹¹⁄₁₆" (18-20mm) tubular nylon webbing; or .315"-¹¹⁄₁₆" (8-20mm) Spectra or Dyneema fiber. (Note that while Dyneema is a trademarked name for a material made from the exact fiber as Spectra, I refer to this material generically as Spectra.) In the manufacturer's strength comparisons, sewn Spectra runners are rated the same as nylon runners. But pound for pound Spectra is ten times stronger than steel: material for bulletproof vests are made from this fiber. Besides being slightly lighter and more durable than nylon, Spectra is highly resistant to UV rays, chemicals, and abrasion, and has a low water-absorption rate. Despite such impressive statistics, Spectra runners are not as versatile, particularly in self-rescue applications.

Although I like the durability of the sewn Spectra runner, I also like the versatility of standard webbing. For tied runners, use tubular nylon webbing. Never cut runners made from Spectra and tie them with knots; its

Creating a tripled quickdraw from a standard shoulder-length runner

You can make your extra-long runners compact for carrying on a single carabiner by doubling and twisting them.

coefficient of friction is too low to hold a knot efficiently. Spectra should only be sewn. With a surface less slippery than Spectra, standard webbing is more effective when used for friction hitches in self-rescue scenarios, and more likely to stay put on natural features that have been runnered.

Sewn quickdraws and runners are made by industrial machines joining webbing or other materials together with sewn rows of zigzags called "bar tacks." Sewn runners offer somewhat greater strength than tied versions, since a knot slightly weakens it while bar tacking doesn't. Yet, stitches can deteriorate with constant abrasion and extensive use, so assess them regularly as they age.

Although somewhat bulkier, tied runners have some benefits over sewn slings. While not an ideal placement, knots on tied runners can serve as protection in a pinch when slotted appropriately in a crack.[5] They can also be untied and retied to more easily bolster manky *rappel stations*, without the hassle of cutting and sacrificing a more expensive nylon sewn sling. Finally, should you need to, you can untie several tied runners to retie one giant one.

To tie a runner, use either a ring bend (aka water) knot or a double fisherman's (grapevine) knot. Consult Chapter 8 for instructions. A double fisherman's takes more webbing to tie, but, once tightened, will rarely loosen on its own. The ring bend requires less webbing to tie but wiggles loose more readily, especially when freshly tied. The ring bend is also a bit bulkier than the slender double fisherman's, but works better for slotting into cracks. Always leave at least a 4" (10cm) tail at each end of the knot. To create one shoulder-length runner you'll need 63" (157.5cm) of tubular webbing. Constantly monitor your tied slings to ensure the knots remain secure. Because new webbing is slippery, it can easily come untied before it's weighted.

RESOURCES

Many resources exist to help you make informed gear choices—so that you fully understanding the pros and cons of what's on the market before you buy. Besides the generalized resources listed below, professional rock guides can help you choose gear for your needs; if you take a rock course, pick your instructor's brain for recommendations.

Magazines

Climbing magazines offer articles and reviews on the latest climbing products and guidebooks. *Climbing's* annual "Gear Guide" is a comprehensive resource with comparison charts covering a variety of new rock tools. Items not covered in the guide generally appear in other issues of *Climbing* or in *Rock & Ice*, sometimes in the form of reviews. Unfortunately, most of the items reviewed are limited to new products because old gear isn't news.

Internet Sites

Several Web sites offer criteria for choosing gear, and host forums where climbers can offer their own assessments. Just beware of e-tailers "reviewing" the gear they sell: these are advertisements masquerading as reviews. Yet some e-tail sites *do* have valuable generalized information.

Catalogs & Advertising

For detailed technical information on strength ratings and testing, refer to manufacturers' catalogs and Web sites. Some catalogs (including Fish Products' online one) have evolved over the years into being more technical resources than simple marketing tools, providing some of the most reliable and current information available. Some manufacturers, for example Petzl, even use paid advertisement space as a forum to share valuable technical information.

Chapter 4

Building a Solid Foundation

Once you're outfitted, the urge to start leading routes can be overwhelming. Take your time; the rock's not going anywhere and there is a lot to learn. Before leading, focus on building a solid foundation of trad skills with a mentor and a reliable partner in low-risk settings.

CLIMBING PARTNERSHIPS

The Ideal Team

Choose your traditional climbing partners with care. Find climbers with similar goals, interests, and abilities. When partners' skill levels are unbalanced, opportunities for individual growth are limited. The less experienced partner never steps into the leadership role and the more skillful climber never learns from someone stronger.

Look for partners who are stable, responsible, and have their egos in check. Those with whom you choose to join forces on traditional routes—particularly long ones—must be honest about their limitations before leaving the ground. Beware of climbers who boast exces-

Heidi Pesterfield

51

sively about their accomplishments or disparage fellow climbers. While these folks generally have talent, their overconfidence, which sometimes covers insecurities, often promotes overstepping true ability levels. Likewise, humility and modesty often mask real strength.

Trust & Mutual Respect

Gear-leading requires continuous problem-solving and decision-making that can be harmonious with the right partner or a power struggle with the wrong one. Respect between partners is of utmost importance. Without trusting your partner's abilities, you soon find yourself at odds with one another. With mutual respect trust is rarely an issue. Duties are shared intuitively, tasks are completed efficiently, and the climb unfolds naturally and safely. "The sum of two partners' energy, wisdom, and strength of will—when those partners are well adapted to each other after years of stress and adventure—is far greater than their individual power and spirit," says Marc Twight in *Extreme Alpinism*. He adds, "It's equally true that two partners who needle each other, who are not aligned in their ambitions or talents, are collectively weaker than they would be on their own."

Couple Partnerships

Climbing with spouses or partners *can* work, but expect a few more psychological hurdles than you'd encounter with others. Partners in romance usually share a sense of comfort that encourages emotional vulnerability. While that's not necessarily a bad thing, sometimes—particularly when one climber is stronger than the other—couples find the emotional climate intensified on a climb. Distracting and counterproductive emotions may erupt. In climbing situations many couples can end up arguing when, in reality, one partner is simply afraid.

Usually, conflicts between couples occur when the route is beyond one partner's abilities. With a boyfriend I've been the weaker climber, scared out of mind, scratching and clawing my way up difficult routes. I've also been the stronger climber, dragging a terrified, inexperienced boyfriend up tricky routes on which I wouldn't have taken a client. Before climbing with your partner in romance, be sure your goals are in sync. If you engage in shouting matches mid-climb, before you climb again devise a simple conflict-resolution process that, by acknowledging fear, works for both parties. Drawn-out tensions rapidly overshadow the positive energy that fuels safe and successful ventures.

Even if you opt for a couple partnership, try climbing with others, too—particularly with members of the same sex. You'll experience a different dynamic that might help you recognize and dissolve any unhealthy pattern that develops by climbing exclusively with your spouse. For example, a woman who has learned everything from her more-experienced boyfriend may not feel comfortable taking on the leadership role. By climbing with another, equally skilled partner, she gets the opportunity. If this partner is another woman, she will probably feel even more empowered.

Climbing With Strangers

Whenever possible, obtain partner recommendations from climbers whom you trust. At some point, though, you may find yourself partnering with a complete stranger. By doing so you risk climbing with those feigning a higher skill level than they actually possess. Hundreds of feet above ground level you don't want to find yourself with some poser whose careless bumbling doesn't square with the grandiose picture he or she painted in the parking lot. Avoid partnering with anyone with a cavalier attitude—*Oh it'll be easy* are famous last words. Also beware of the Jekyll and Hyde partners are gentle as lambs on the ground, but transform into seething hyenas on the rock. Because you may not have the skills to extricate yourself from such unfortunate situations as a beginner, do proper assessments of potential partners on the ground.

Though it's always a gamble, climbing with a stranger can be a good experience. Perhaps because you feel comfortable exposing weaknesses to those you know best, in the presence of those you know least you can put your best foot forward. Work out any kinks in your partnership on a short route far below your ability levels, or at a top-rope site. Climbers from different regions often perform tasks slightly differently—be it a particular com-

Climber: Abby Watkins

Years Trad Free Climbing: 13

Average Trad Lead Ability: 5.12

Favorite Trad Climbing Area(s):
Arapiles and Moonarie (Australia),
Yosemite, the Bugaboos (Canada),
& Indian Creek

Most Respected Trad Free Climber:
Louise Shepard

A Blessing and a Curse

A woman alone on the road is fairly unusual in North America, yet we climbers often pack our cars to the gills and head off to some grand and beautiful mountain setting without a partner. For years I traveled the North American continent in my Honda Accord hatchback, pulling into climbing areas and finding random partners whenever I could. It was a blessing and a curse—though some of my best partners (now best friends) were among those strangers, I had some odd experiences, too.

—Like backing off The Nose on El Cap after struggling up eight pitches, having led six myself and watching in woe while my partner took three hours to lead his. In my experience men have often overstated their abilities when we talk in the parking lot. I became wary after that, and made sure I was pre-

pared to do all of the leading if necessary. A few years later I ended up leading the whole of the Steck/-Salathe (also in Yosemite Valley) with another guy. He seemed to have credentials in the parking lot, but after the first pitch he said I should keep leading. To his credit he realized that to complete the climb before dark we needed to move fast, and that he wasn't up to it. It turned out to be an excellent day, and I really enjoyed leading pitch after pitch after pitch. But, if I hadn't the skills to lead the remaining pitches, the situation would have had the makings of an epic.

These experiences didn't stop me from climbing with strangers though, and I'm grateful they didn't. Some years later I ran into a young guy who was climbing pretty well around the Valley. After he sug-

Continued on next page

gested we do Astroman, we racked up for this classic and flew up it in half a day, sharing responsibilities equally. A few days later we added the cream by cruising The Nose in a day. These are two of the most rewarding and memorable climbing experiences I've had in Yosemite.

Climbing puts you into very intense situations that depend on these partnerships. From relation- ships coming together out of nowhere but making me trust another with my life, I've learned much about myself and gained new insights about others. I've also learned to be thoroughly self-suffi- cient in my climbing—something I might have missed if I hadn't struck out on my own.

—Abby Watkins

mand, a belay method, or an anchoring technique. Before you commit to a route challenging your limits, assess a new partner's skills and methods, and, even at the last minute, don't be afraid to back out.

Mentors

Find a knowledgeable trad specialist willing to con- sistently spend time with you at the crags, and make that person your mentor. Or hire a guide. In either case, express your interest in learning everything they're will- ing to teach you. If you find someone with the patience and tolerance to fill this role, be open to every learning opportunity as it occurs: observe carefully, ask questions, and then practice what you've learned with other climbers at your own level. In medical school it's com- mon practice for students to learn procedures in a three- part system: watch one, do one, and then teach one. This is a terrific way for climbers to share knowledge.

PROTECTION PLACEMENT

Cornerstone of the trad leading experience is the slow but gratifying process of learning to place reliable protection. Take time to carefully study anchors and gear placement long before you take the sharp end, and pay close attention while following trad pitches. If you skimp on this phase of learning, you're doing yourself and

Climber: **Doug Robinson**

Years Trad Free Climbing: **43**

Average Trad Free Climbing Lead
    Ability: **5.10+/5.11-**

Favorite Trad Climbing Area: **High Sierra**

Most Respected Trad Free Climber:
    Chuck Pratt

Jim Harrington

How Can I Trust My Placements?

You can't. Not at first. So don't expect to stake your life on them right away.

Trusting your placements is tough because it's a judgment of a technique. The technique is hard enough: take a few very simple tools, light alloy wedges, all sizes, and families of spring-open cams, and fit them into cracks in rock, infinitely varied in shape. Simple tools, complex and ever-changing application. And there's no practical way to spot-test placements, not for the tonnage of force you want, and may need, them to hold.

You need judgment. But how are you going to get it? Pro falls squarely into that danger zone where, as they say, "We get too soon good, and too late smart." It is far easier to learn to slot pieces into cracks than to decide how much they can be trusted.

Judging your pro is one of those cruxes in your climbing career where you need help, either from an experienced mentor or a professional instructor. As a guide, protection and anchoring is one of my favorite subjects to teach. It's a big opportunity to help someone's climbing leap into new realms. The challenge is to go there while maintaining a margin of safety.

What I do is actually pretty simple. Students each take a rack and place all the pieces from the ground. Then the whole class goes over each placement, and I discuss what's good, where it could be better, and how I know. Then we do it again before going on to combining individual placements into a SERENE anchor.

—Doug Robinson

future partners a great disservice. Be diligent and commit yourself to excellence.

Ground Work

The best place to learn protection placement is from the safety of the ground. Visit local climbing areas and practice placing hardware along the base of the crags. Take along an experienced gear-leader and ask for feedback. While this book provides basic guidelines, guidance from an experienced leader or a class will benefit you most.

Rock Integrity

A protection placement is only as stable as the integrity of the rock surrounding it. When considering each placement location, first evaluate the rock. Thump on the area with the palm of your hand and listen. If you hear a hollow sound, the rock is partially detached from the main wall, perhaps to the degree that the force of a fall would tear it completely off. In this unfortunate scenario your protection is gone, and you, your partner, and the rope run the risk of being injured by rockfall.

Evaluate a crack by its depth and texture. If it looks shallow and feels particularly granular and crumbly, seek out another placement location: you don't want your piece too close to the opening, or resting on unstable crystals or nubbins that could break under force. Finally, choose a crack placement away from other intersecting fractures. Even small fractures can undermine an otherwise stable crack's integrity.

Stoppers/Nuts

Stoppers and nuts are designed to slot or wedge into tapered cracks, with as much surface area touching the rock as possible. When force is applied, a Stopper's wedging action is initiated. If the rock is strong enough to withstand the force, the tighter the wedge becomes.

For an ideal Stopper placement seek out a V-shaped narrowing constriction in the rock *(Photo: right)*. With the wired stem of the Stopper in line with the anticipated load direction, slot your placement and give it one hearty tug. The placement should resist a downward pull by wedging into the slot. If you have a choice, place a

A Stopper placement wedged securely into a bottleneck constriction in the crack

This SLCD is too small for this crack

medium or large Stopper instead of a smaller micro-stopper (under 6mm or ¼"). This is wise particularly at the beginning of a lead, where forces on your piece are generally greater. Tiny Stoppers lack the strength bigger ones afford. When placing micros, also consider the type of rock on which you're climbing. Steel nuts are stronger than some rocks, increasing the chance that the rock will shatter under force (see Chapter 3).

SLCDs

"Life is good. As climbers, we now enjoy a wide variety of plug-and-go protection. Even better, the technology has been around long enough that the designs are thoroughly tweaked for the best performance, durability, and price," says Clyde Soles[6]. True, but without the skills to place a cam correctly, you benefit little from the technology, warns longtime climber and professional guide Scott Cosgrove: "Cams are not the cure-all or end-all. They are easily misused even by very experienced climbers. Get a guide or experienced climber with a long track record to show you placement guidelines early in your leading career."

All SLCDs function by the same basic mechanical principle: in short, each individual cam pushes out against the rock when force is applied to the stem. With all their moving parts, SLCD placements can dislodge or walk with relative ease. A correctly placed SLCD has its stem oriented in the anticipated load-bearing direction. Holding power is optimal if every cam on the device is retracted at mid-expansion range—no one cam more than another. If the cams of the unit you placed are more than halfway open, try the next larger size (Photos: 1 and 2, left). An SLCD too small for a placement is prone to walking due to rope movement, and to potentially opening in an inverted (or tipped) position (although many new SLCDs have cam stops designed to avoid the latter). Yet, if you overstuff an SLCD too large for a crack, your partner will have trouble removing it.

Because of their limited expansion range, micro cams (under 1") are usually placed beyond mid-expansion—up to 90 percent. These tiny units have less holding strength than most larger-sized cams, so save them for tricky placements when option are few. Likewise

The correct size SLCD for the same crack

choose a 4-cam over a 3-cam unit for most applications—the 4-cam almost always offers superior holding power, and tends to be more stable because it is wider and moves around less after placement.

Because of an SLCD's potential for walking, consider the morphology of the rock around a proposed placement. If a crack widens above or behind your placement, the cams can fully or partially open, after the device walks due to rope friction. *(Photos: 1 and 2, right)*. Look instead for a potential placement with constrictions above and behind to prevent its walking *(Photo: next page, top left)*. While relatively simple in theory, SLCD placement can befuddle climbers new to cam-craft. When placing a cam your focus often narrows such that you don't take in the surrounding area. Before making a placement ask yourself, *Where might the device walk?*

Here are a few special considerations for SLCD placement. A flared crack wider at the lip that becomes gradually narrower with depth is very difficult to protect with an SLCD, or any gear. Though offset SLCDs sometimes offer a solution, most new leaders don't own these specialty pieces. Often the only decent cam placement is one deep inside where the crack is narrowest, and possibly slightly more parallel. Horizontal cracks offer great placements for SLCDs with flexible stems. Though rigid-stem cams (like forged Friends) can be rigged with additional materials to work in horizontals, they are best reserved for placement in vertical cracks. Note that mud, dirt, ice, and snow, which reduce friction inside cracks, compromise the

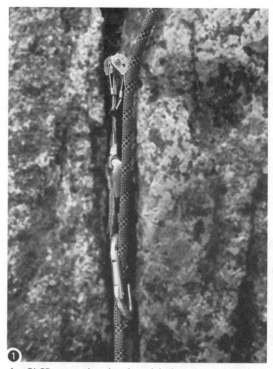

❶ An SLCD precariously placed below a section that widens above it.

❷ The same SLCD after having "walked" into the space above it. This piece would definitely not hold a fall.

An ideally placed SLCD below a chockstone to prevent walking

A Hexcentric placement that utilizes its camming capability

holding power of all SLCDs. On particularly soft rock, place each cam beyond mid-expansion range but below 90%; this helps prevent the possibility of the unit "skating" out of the crack.

Hexcentrics & Tri-Cams

When loaded, Black Diamond Hexcentrics and Lowe Tri-Cams are designed to lock into place by a slight camming or rotational action. Tapered slots are excellent for utilizing the cam action of a Hex *(Photo: bottom left)*. For optimal camming placement, the sling (or wire) should be off-center. These devices can also be wedged into cracks like Stoppers *(Photo: opposite page, top right)*. Neither are exceptional for protection in a flared crack.

In a slightly irregular crack secure a good Tri-Cam placement with the point resting in a slight depression or shelf, and the rounded side against the opposite side of the crack. The sling is designed to run along the length of the curved side so that when weighted downward, the sharp side cams into place *(Photo: opposite page, bottom right)*.

Bolts

To many rock climbers the fixed bolt is viewed as security. In the sport climbing world, bolts are clipped thoughtlessly and often with great relief. Yet many of the bolts on traditional routes are not safe. Most older bolts *(Illustration: top of page 62)*, which tend to be ¼" (6mm) relics with low strength ratings, can shear with relative ease. Back them up with a piece off your rack whenever possible. More trustworthy are an assortment of modern ⅜-½" (0.95-1.25cm) expansion bolts, as well as the hearty Petzl Glue-In bolt *(Illustration: bottom of page 62)*. With strength ratings upwards of 4000 lbs (8818kg), these are safe if they're in good shape and have been placed correctly.

All bolts are subject to improper placement. A well-placed expansion bolt lies flush against solid rock without evidence of rock cratering (or chipping) around the base, which indicates a poor placement. Bolt hangers should be stationary and free from obvious damage or rust. Some internal errors include: overtightening the Wedge bolt, rock dust interfering with tightening of the

Rawl bolt, and improper curing of the Petzl Glue-In. Besides curing time, the quality of the Glue-In is also affected by hole diameter, humidity levels, and temperatures. Bolts less than ½" (1.25cm) are unreliable in soft rock such as sandstone. Unfortunately, these internal placement errors are undetectable by subsequent climbers. Nevertheless, understand potential errors so that you don't worship the bolt as an infallible piece of equipment. Use your best judgment, trust gut feelings, and back up any bolts that you suspect won't provide optimal strength.

Natural Pro

Natural protection is my personal favorite. Every time I find a natural feature I can lasso for protection I feel like Mother Nature and I have outsmarted technology with some simple, down-to-earth innovation. No animals were harmed or tested with my slinging a natural horn for pro, and no sweatshop labor was relied upon with my using the big, friendly girth of a Jeffrey pine as part of my anchor system.

A Hexcentric wedged into a crack like a Stopper

Though artificial climbing gadgets deserve high praise, don't miss the opportunities that natural pro affords. Always look out for sturdy horns, *chicken heads*, *huecos* (holes), tunnels, *chockstones*, trees, or flakes for use as protection. You won't have to use a piece off your rack—a plus if you're conserving gear on lead. To secure a sling through a small hueco, or around a small chicken head, tree, rock tunnel, or chockstone, use a girth hitch (see Chapter 8) *(Illustrations: 1-3, top of page 63 / Photos: 1 and 2, bottom of page 63).*

To prevent a pulley effect, avoid using the girth hitch on larger objects. Instead, use a large runner (or two girth hitched together) draped over the top of the object and joined at its base with a carabiner *(Photo: top of page 64).* Lacking these resources, untie one or two of your tied runners and retie them together around the object, completely encircling it. Either way, make sure your sling(s) are long enough to avoid dangerous load multiplication. Lacking these resources, use a double bowline knot if you are setting up a belay and have adequate rope available. If you're slinging a horn or a flake, be certain it has a stable connection to the main rock, and loop your run-

A small Tri-Cam placed in a crack

Older bolts with low strength ratings

1) ¹/₄″ Compression/button, 2) ¹/₄″ Compression/nut, 3) Self-drill Expansion,
4) Nail Star-Drive, 5) Torque Bolt, 6) Zamac Nail-In

Modern bolts with high (upwards of 4000 lbs.) strength ratings

1) Fixe Wedge, 2) Rawl 5-Piece, 3) Petzl Long-life, 4) Petzl Glue-In

Natural Protection

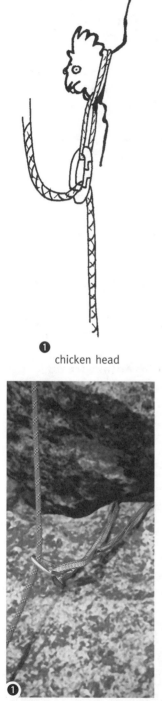

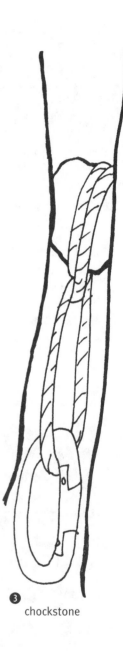

① chicken head

② huecos

③ chockstone

1) A rock tunnel secured with a threaded sling

2) A small tree secured with a girthed sling

A large tree secured with two girthed slings draped around it and joined at the base with carabiners

ner as close to the plinth as possible. If, having looped a sling over a shallow feature, you're worried the rope movement can lift the sling off, add the weight of a spare cam or even a water bottle to prevent it from happening. Or, if your sling is long enough, secure it snugly with an overhand slipknot or a *clove hitch* and a carabiner. Slings made from standard webbing offer better-adhering, tackier surfaces than do those made of slippery Spectra.

Carabiner Use

Loads should only weight a carabiner across its vertical axis (lengthwise). Never place a 'biner so that could be loaded horizontally—across its gate and spine *(Photo: left)*. Known as "cross-loading," this practice reduces a carabiner's strength by 50%. Also avoid placing a carabiner where it's weighted over an edge; under very low loads it could break.

"Of all the gear you use, carabiners suffer the most failures.... The problem isn't defective gear—it's because all of the things that can happen to a 'biner during a fall, resulting in an open gate...or accidental unclipping," say the editors of the June 1999 issue of *Rock & Ice* No. 93. If a load weights a carabiner at the moment its gate is open, failure can occur. Collision with natural objects can force gates open, as can the vibration of a rope during a fall. Keep the gate openings of carabiners facing away from the rock, and prevent clothing and other equipment (particularly home-tied runner tails) from interfering with gate closure. Avoid linking two or more carabiners together, which can unclip from each other with ease. Instead, create extensions with slings whenever possible. Also, carabiners can easily come unclipped from the rope on lead protection, unless you avoid the practice of "back-clipping" (see Chapter 5).

An improperly placed carabiner at risk of being horizontally "cross-loaded"

Locking carabiners are best reserved for *primary links* in your system, while standard non-lockers suffice for *secondary links*. A primary link doesn't have a backup; should it fail, you're a goner. Primary links that utilize lockers include: your belay/rappel device, clipping into anchors at belays, and use at the *masterpoint* on any anchor. Many self-rescue techniques also involve primary links where locking carabiners are a must. Lockers might also be used on lead to clip critical pieces that could prevent a potentially devastating fall. In a pinch—in lieu of a locker—use two reversed and opposed 'biners *(Photo: top right)*.

Two reversed and opposed 'biners

Multidirectional Placements

Climbers new to trad climbing have little experience with multidirectional placements, which are set to withstand upward, lateral, and downward forces. Climbers use them most commonly as an anchor component on a multipitch route, although other circumstances (discussed in Chapter 5) may also require their use. Bolts or horizontal SLCD placements offer obvious multidirectional protection, as do some natural features (like a good-sized tree). Since these placements aren't always available, you can create a multidirectional configuration by coupling two opposing unidirectional pieces. Place the upper one to accept a downward force, and the lower one to accept an upward force. Join the two pieces with a sling held in place with a snug clove hitch (see Chapter 8). This is called an *oppositional placement* (*Photo: bottom right*).

Join two unidirectional pieces with a sling and clove hitch to create an oppositional placement for multidirectional use.

Many leaders rely on vertically placed SLCDs as multidirectionals, expecting them to rotate and accommodate other directional forces. They can and will—sometimes. Since a cam is unstable when it rotates, failure is always a possibility. While you can't *completely* trust the unit during or after rotation, on the other hand, forces should be relatively low when a piece like this might be weighted—it's a judgment call.

ANCHORS

Once you've mastered the basics of gear placement, you can turn your attention toward learning to create anchor systems. Anchor building involves creativity and ingenuity, and can be a lot of fun. During the learning process, remain at the base of the crags, under the watchful eye of your mentor or a qualified instructor.

The Pre-Equalized Anchor System

The ideal anchoring method for new leaders is what is known as a pre-equalized system using a tied cordelette or sewn Web-o-lette™. Introduced to the American professional guiding community by their Canadian peers in the late 1980s, this comprehensive system has since become popular for recreational climbers.

The pre-equalized anchor system has many advantages not found in other systems. Best of all, it distributes the force of a load among all components, and prevents shock-loading should any one piece fail. These are two key features of the common *SERENE* mnemonic used in anchor craft.

This system is also ideal on lead because, relying on the cordelette, it doesn't eat up valuable rope (critical on multipitch routes involving long pitches); it eliminates

---

SERENE Anchor Checklist

Use the SERENE mnemonic as a mental checklist to build bomber anchors. Ask yourself the following questions, and make sure the answer to each is affirmative:

S=Safe. Is your gear placed correctly in solid rock? Are fixed pieces (bolts and pitons) and natural features of excellent quality?

E=Equalized. When weighted, does each anchor component share the load equally?

R=Redundant. Is each component of the anchor backed up at least once?

E=Easy. Is your anchor simple? Does it avoid complicated arrangements and unnecessary gear?

NE=No Extension. If one component of the anchor fails, does your arrangement assure that no other component will be *shock-loaded*?

the need to conserve multiple slings for the belay. Establishment is, however, time consuming, and requires additional gear (the cordelette or Web-o-lette™).

Three Piece Minimum

For climbers in their early years of anchor building a good rule of thumb is: **No matter how solid you think your pieces are, don't place less than three.** Obviously exceptions exist. If your can belay off a sturdy, sufficiently rooted, live tree, one is sufficient. Also, an anchor consisting of two *bomber* bolts is usually adequate.

Redundancy

Create additional redundancy in your anchor system by utilizing more than one rock feature for protection, whenever possible. For instance, when several cracks are available, use two. Should something occur to one feature that reduced its reliability, your anchor is backed up with another.

Force Multiplication

Anchor physics are such that the system load varies in proportion to the angle formed by any two components. When angles of the joined gear components are less than 60 degrees, the anchor system is safest. Anything greater than 60 degrees exponentially multiplies the force bearing on your pieces, endangering the system *(Sidebar: following page).*

Think of the triangle formed between the masterpoint and any two anchor components as a slice of pizza: the larger the slice, the more load each piece must bear. A worst-case scenario would be loading the center of a taut horizontal sling between two level anchors. If one of your anchor pieces is off in right or left field, link it to the main system with extra slings to decrease the angle *(Photos: 1 and 2, page 69).*

Climbers new to anchor craft frequently are confused about when and where to use a locking carabiner. Many overcompensate by using a locker at every link. Yet a carabiner linking a single piece of protection (or bolt) to a multi-component anchoring system is generally a secondary link. Only the masterpoint—the primary link—on a Web-o-lette™ or cordelette anchor re-

Force Multiplication

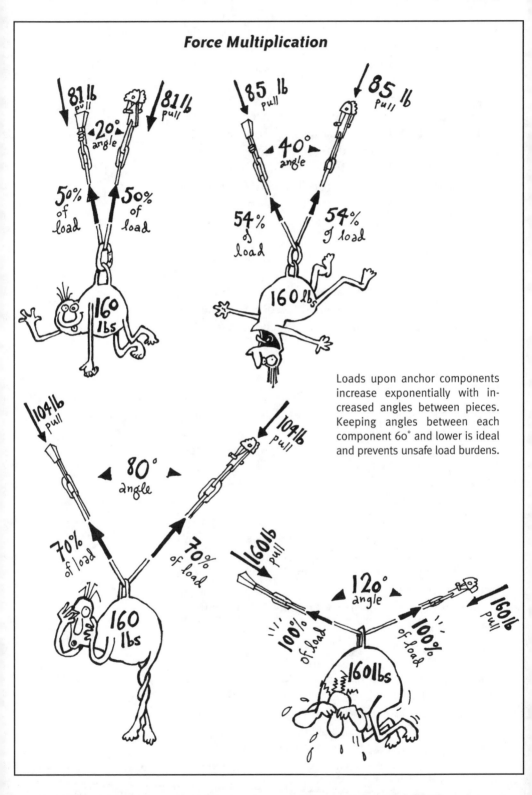

Loads upon anchor components increase exponentially with increased angles between pieces. Keeping angles between each component 60° and lower is ideal and prevents unsafe load burdens.

Decrease Angles, Increase Safety

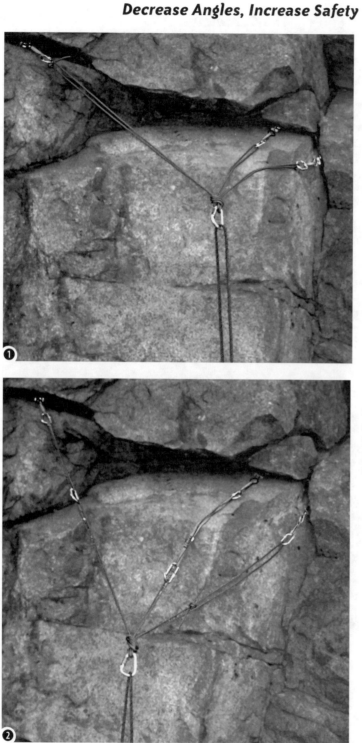

Angles created by corde-lette between two pieces are too large, potential-ly requiring each piece to tolerate nearly 80% of the load.

Correct this dilemma by adding longer slings to the middle and highest pieces, decreasing the angle to around 50%.

The Cordelette

To assemble a pre-equalized anchor system using a cordelette, follow these steps:

1. Clip all three pieces of protection with single carabiners and attach your cordelette to form a giant circle connecting them all together.

2. Form two bights in the rope, one between each piece. Simultaneously pull these two bights down to join the bottom loop of the cordelette, ensuring that each strand meets precisely at the exact same point, thereby equalizing the future load between all three pieces.

Continued on next page

3. Decide the exact direction of the anticipated load, and adjust the cordelette so that all anchor points will share the load. To easily accomplish this, place your thumb in the loops created by the gathered bights and, while pulling downward, slide it from side to side until you've accommodated the determined load direction. This must be done with absolute precision or the load will not be shared by all of your pieces.

4. With your other hand, grasp all of the strands tightly above the gathered bights and, keeping your thumb in place, carefully slide this hand toward the anchors *(Photo: 4a)* until you can tie an overhand knot. Be certain to keep all of the strands together as you tie the knot, and allow space in the loop for at least two locking carabiners. *(Photo: 4b)* The knot functions to prevent extension and shock-loading of any one piece in the system should any others fail. The loops below the knot are both clipped as your masterpoint, where you anchor at belay stations, or thread a rope to create a top-rope.

The Web-o-lette™

To help beginners with the Web-o-lette™ assembly, Mountain Tools has created a simple equation: V+W+8=On Belay!:

1. Clip all three pieces of protection with single carabiners, and clip each sewn loop end of the Web-o-lette™ into the carabiners on the two far ends forming a V.

2. Clip the center of the bight between the ends to your middle piece, forming a W.

3. Form two loops of equal length by gathering these bights together and tying a figure 8, to create your masterpoint.

quires a locker. Although one locking carabiner is adequate here, use two at the masterpoint of any anchor you cannot monitor visually. Examples include the anchors of systems managed from below such as yo-yo top-ropes and rappels. When the masterpoint can be easily monitored, single lockers are sufficient.

Anchors & Load Direction

Anchor systems are either multidirectional or unidirectional, depending on the anticipated load direction. New leaders should practice building both.

Unidirectional Anchors

Unidirectional anchors need only accommodate a force in one direction and include the following types of applications:

• An anchor to resist a downward force on the top of a single-pitch route or atop the final pitch of a multipitch route.

• A base anchor established to accommodate an upward force on the first pitch of a route beginning from the ground. (This optional anchor is discussed in Chapter 5.)

• A rappel anchor, almost always fixed (established by the first ascent party) usually needs to resist only a downward force. Fixed yo-yo toprope anchors are also usually unidirectional.

Multidirectional Anchors

Where you need to accommodate upward, lateral, and downward forces, your anchor must be multidirectional. (At least one component must withstand upward and lateral forces.) The multidirectional anchor is used at all multipitch belays, with the exception of the final pitch and sometimes the first.

Upward and/or lateral forces in the multipitch scenario (described in Chapter 6) occur during standard leader falls where, because at least one of the leader's pieces holds, the belayer at

A multidirectional belay anchor withstanding upward and lateral forces

the anchor below experiences upward and/or lateral tension while braking the fall *(Illustration: page 73)*. A downward force occurs when the follower falls after having been belayed at the anchor above by the leader. *(Illustration: left)* A downward force also occurs if the leader falls before placing a piece of protection when climbing above the anchor, or if this piece or all lead pieces fail, resulting in a fall past the belayer. *(Also illustrated at left.)*

The component of a multidirectional anchor set to accommodate an upward and/or lateral force should be placed low in your cordelette/Web-o-lette™ configuration, since the higher this piece is (in falls with significant upward force) the more distance you can be lifted. If this component is a unidirectional piece, consider securing it with an oppositional piece.

Potential downward forces on multipitch anchors are always greater. The maximum upward force on a multidirectional anchor is subtler; it's determined by the amount of friction in the system. (Fall forces are discussed at length in Chapter 6.) Generally, the more rope in use and the more pieces placed by the leader, the less force on the belayer and anchor. Consequently, you need only one upward force placement as a component of most multidirectional anchors.

Fixed Anchors

Although never guaranteed, you may encounter fixed belay anchors on a route. Expect fixed anchors only when indicated in guidebooks. Rappel routes are always fixed, having been preestablished by first-ascent parties where walk-offs are not possible. The quality of a fixed anchor can vary. **Just because it's there doesn't mean it's safe.** Bolts, pitons, and natural features are the most common components of fixed anchors. Before using one, evaluate the integrity of the placements and the rock. Avoid antiquated rusting pitons with broken eyeholes, and check natural features for stability. If a natural feature appears loose, do not use it.

A multidirectional belay anchor withstanding a downward force

If any other component is questionable, back it up with a piece from your rack.

Many fixed anchor configurations exist, some better than others *(Illustrations: 1-4, right)*. Use your knowledge regarding appropriate angles, equalizing and shock-loading possibilities to determine the quality of configuration. Chains or webbing link components of a fixed rappel anchor. Since some belay anchors double as rappel stations, you may encounter such anchors during your ascent. When belaying, don't clip into the masterpoint of such anchors. Instead, clip directly into each individual piece and create your own pre-equalized configuration with a cordelette or a Web-o-lette™.

Never belay off open *or* closed *cold shuts* *(Photo: page 76)*. These soft-metal hardware-store "anchors" rated poorly in unofficial 1997 strength tests and cannot withstand high loads. Primarily found on top of sport routes, cold shuts are suited only for static, low-load tasks (like lowering a climber after a lead). Do not, however, use them as rappel anchors unless they have been hammered completely shut. Even then, I might back up a cold shut with a piece from my rack.

Rappel anchors are always fixed so climbers can retrieve ropes without leaving behind their own gear. Individual rappel anchor components are joined by either chain links or webbing. If necessary, cut away weathered nests of discolored, stiff, and/or abraded webbing and replace with webbing from one of your own tied runners. Check the masterpoint for redundancy, rust, and grooving, and replace or bolster with either a *rappel ring* or carabiner from your rack. Finally, check the anchor for appropriate equalization and make alterations with webbing (again, from tied runners off your rack) if necessary.

Fixed Anchor Configurations

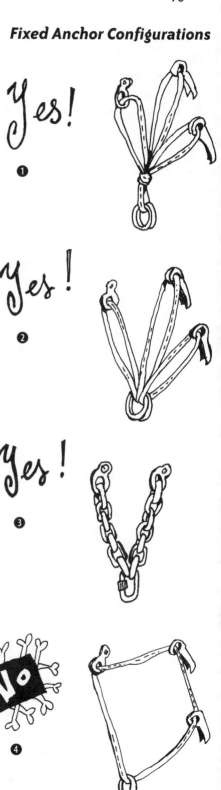

The cold shut rates poorly in strength tests

Other Anchoring Methods

Pre-equalizing with a cordelette is just one of many anchoring methods. Effective anchors can also be built without cordelettes using your rope. Although only one of these methods is described in Chapter 8, several others exist. Many require more advanced protection placement skills and keener judgment than the new leader possesses. With more overall experience on the rock, you will benefit from learning additional techniques. Intermediate leaders should refer to John Long's book, *Anchors*, and John Long and Bob Gaines' *More Anchors*.

NAVIGATION AIDS

Together with other resources, guidebooks and topographical (*topo*) drawings provide guidance for exploring new climbing areas and getting up and down routes. *Beta* is more specific information gleaned from other climbers.

Guidebooks

In a well-written guidebook the introduction contains information about a particular area's human as well as climbing history. It also lists optimal climbing seasons for that area, camping information, and hazards to be aware of (rattlesnakes, poison oak or ivy, loose rock, climbing on fragile rock shortly after rain). It describes any pertinent area rules and regulations and regional climbing ethics. A few examples include: power drills are not allowed in national parks like Yosemite; most crags in North Carolina welcome only traditional, ground-up ascents; Devils Tower in Wyoming is closed to climbing for one month in the summer to honor a Native American tradition; and, many cliffs throughout the US are closed for certain months to accommodate nesting raptors. By honoring requests like these, climbers maintain favor with land managers, conservationists, and local climbers.

The main section of a climbing guidebook usually features topo renderings of established area routes, and sometimes includes narrative descriptions and photographs. Though limited in use, photos can help you identify landmark features like roofs, corners, and ledge systems. Narratives provide fine complements for topos, but by themselves are vague and often confusing. Interestingly, when topos came onto the climbing scene in the 1970s, some viewed their use as "cheating."[7]

Topos *(Sidebar: pages 78 and 79)*

Topography is defined as the "detailed, graphic representation of the surface features of a place...indicating relative positions and elevations." Although climbing topos do not resemble maps with contour lines used for hiking and backpacking, they accomplish a similar task of guiding adventurers through vertiginous terrain. Guidebooks offer legends with fairly standardized symbols used to identify varied features of a rock face. Learning to read climbing topos is a little like learning a new language. To read them you'll need to translate symbols for roofs and overhangs, ledges, corners (dihedrals), faces, straight-in cracks, flares, and chimneys.

Beta

As a new leader, consider supplementing guidebook data with information from additional resources prior to your ascent. Such resources might include friends or acquaintances who have recently been to a particular climbing area or completed a specific route. Also check with qualified local climbing shop personnel. This supplemental information you gather is referred to as beta, which refers affectionately to the late climber Jack Mileski.[8] Obtaining beta for the approach and descent is

---

Topo Literacy

One great drill for becoming topo literate is to study the legend of your local climbing area guidebook, head to the crags with paper and pencil, and then draw your own topo versions of a few routes. Then compare these to the topos of the same routes in the guidebook. Even better, sit down in front of a small boulder and draw a route that represents the miniature features on a short section as if they were full-sized.

TOPO-SCHMOPO 5.8

Climbing guidebooks usually feature any combination of the following navigational data for each route: photo *(below left)*, topo *(below right)*, and narrative description *(opposite page, left)*. [Familiarize yourself with a typical climbing topo by comparing information shown for the fictional route below and on the next page.]

Continued on next page

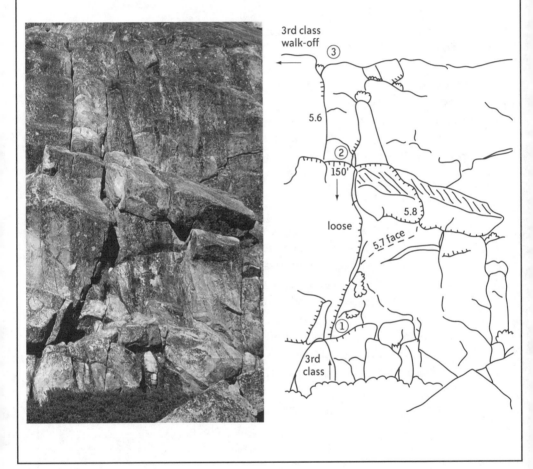

Narrative Description

PITCH 1: Scramble up third class boulders to a ledge at the base of an obvious right-facing dihedral.

PITCH 2: Climb the corner past a large bush and surmount an oblong chockstone. Traversing right, face climb (5.7) below an overhang to the base of a short finger crack splitting a small roof. Proceed over the roof (5.8) and across a ramp leading to a ledge. Move 10´ left and belay at the base of an obvious hand crack.

PITCH 3: Climb the hand crack (5.6) leading to the final belay ledge.

DESCENT: Scramble south to third class ledge system leading back to the base.

Common Topo Legend

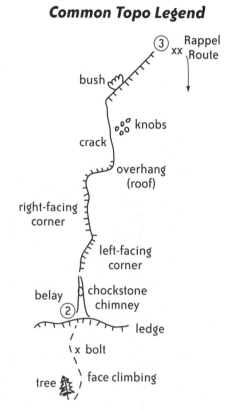

also crucial. In this country, United States Geological Survey (USGS) maps can be helpful, particularly for backcountry routes with long and/or complex approaches and descents.

While guidebooks, topos, and beta are all valuable tools, only a portion of reality can be conveyed through maps, drawings, and friends' descriptions. No matter how detailed, these resources have limitations. Sometimes routes won't live up to the guidebook's description, or your interpretation of it. Some topos are vague or even wrong. In other instances, you may strongly disagree with the published rating of a particular climb. To avoid frustration and disappointment, come prepared and don't be surprised when the route is something other than your expectation. Equal in value to information gathered before any ascent are being flexible, thinking on your toes, and cultivating good route-finding abilities.

BASIC CRACK CLIMBING

"Historical big walls and free routes of any honest length invariably follow crack systems, so to climb them you must be crack fluent," say authors John Long and Craig Luebben in *Advanced Rock Climbing*. While basic face climbing tends to be intuitive, crack climbing-skills must be learned. If you're new to crack climbing, get inspired by watching a crack master in action: see Dale Bard finessing his way up Coyne Crack in the video *Moving Over Stone II*, or Lisa Gnade on Ruby's Café in *Masters of Stone*. These climbers didn't learn crack technique overnight and neither will you. But once you've devoted several seasons to perfecting your technique, it will gradually begin to come naturally.

Learning how to climb cracks from a book is as unlikely as learning to ride a bike this way; it does little for your crack climbing progress. What results in headway is groveling your way up cracks until you get it right. This kinesthetic process unfolds on the rock. And, like anything, some climbers initially have an easier time with cracks than others. Like learning skiing or snowboarding it may seem difficult at first, but with minor increments of increased competency it becomes more and more enjoyable. Yet you can expect discomfort and awkwardness in the learning process, plus you'll lose a lot of skin, too.

Crack climbing involves *jamming* techniques in which climbers wedge their appendages (hands, fingers, feet, legs, arms, or whatever works) into cracks to create enough purchase to make upward progress. More often than not, you supplement your jams with a combination of other techniques such as face climbing, *smearing*, and *stemming*.

Most climbers new to crack climbing go through a phase thinking they're not strong enough to climb cracks. By lifting weights in fitness facilities they hope to build the strength they think is needed for crack routes. Back at the crags, they are met with yet another brutal and humiliating defeat. If they persevere in practicing outdoors on easy cracks, though, they eventually discover they were lacking in cultivated technique, not strength.

Developing Crack Technique

To develop basic crack technique, begin either by top-roping or by following low-angled crack routes with lots of features. Don't start off on vertical or steeper routes unless they have a lot of face holds. Forget about how hard you can climb on bolted sport routes; cracks rated below 5.8 are recommended for first-timers. Difficulty ratings of cracks compared to bolted clip-ups don't translate well (see Chapter 9).

To initiate any jam, determine the best possible placement a particular section has to offer. The ideal jam might not be obvious, so experiment with different options until you find the right one. Initially, new crack climbers often make the mistake of rejecting bomber jams in favor of face holds outside the crack. Avoiding jams will only prolong the learning process and make the climbing more difficult than its rating. Since your motor memory needs the right information to absorb, focus primarily on utilizing the crack and give yourself over to the jamming action. The more cracks you climb, the more confidence you gain in your jamming skills. And, as the cracks you climb become steeper with less hand- and footholds on the face, the more pure crack technique you are going to rely upon. Eventually you'll discover the advantages (and sometimes the necessity) of using both hands and both feet in the crack simultaneously.

Here are some basic jamming techniques:

Hand Jams: (Photo: right) To initiate a hand jam, look for natural constrictions in the crack around head height that would facilitate wedging your hand in place like a Stopper. With your thumb tucked against your palm, insert your hand into the crack, and locate that sweet spot that, when your hand is flexed, locks it in place. Don't be afraid to fish around for the best fit, and then gently rotate your elbow down and in toward your chest,

Hand jamming

Foot jamming

❶
Finger jamming—thumb up

❷
Finger jamming—thumb down

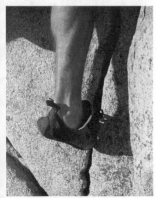

Toe jamming

torquing your hand securely in place. Jams can be executed with the thumbs facing down or up, depending on how much leverage you're going to need to reach the next jam.

Foot Jams: (Photo: top left) The most efficient tool for establishing secure foot and toe jams is your eyesight. Blindly throwing a foot into a crack and expecting it to hold doesn't work. Look down and consciously decide exactly where you're going to place your jam. Find a location in the crack around knee level that is closest to the size of your foot, and constrictions or knobs that may provide added security once your foot's wedged into place. Once you've got your target, gently lift and rotate your lower leg until the inside of your calf is perpendicular to the rock, pinkie toe down and parallel with the crack. Insert your foot. If you've ever played Hacky Sack, this is the same position, with the inside of your foot flattened, you use to keep the sack in flight. Now with as much deliberation as possible, transfer all of your weight to this foot by straightening the knee, allowing it to rotate inward until it is parallel with the crack.

Finger & Toe Jams: For good finger jams, again look for thin cracks with openings that constrict and form V-shaped slots. Insert your fingers (with the exception of your thumb) into the crack, either thumbs up or down, *(Photos 1 and 2: left)* wedging them above the constriction to the best of your ability. It's not always necessary to get each of your fingers in all the way for the jam to be useful. Now rotate your elbow inward and downward, torquing the fingers in place. Toe jams work the same way foot jams do, except you may only be able to get the tips of your toe box into the crack resulting in a hybrid between a smear and a jam *(Photo: bottom left)*.

Fist & Cupped-Hand Jams: Fist jams *(Photo: top right)* are reserved for cracks too wide for a secure hand jam. A fist jam can be executed with the thumb tucked inside your palm or outside, depending on the width of the crack. Wedge it in, and flex. If the crack's a tad too large for tight hand jamming, try a cupped-hand jam. For a cupped-hand jam, make a C shape with your hand, then straighten all of your fingers except your thumb, maintaining the C. Place your open hand inside a crack and flex it *(Photo: middle right)*. These two styles tend to feel a

lot less secure than good hand or finger jams, but with
some practice you'll become comfortable trusting them.

Shuffling & Crossing Over

The best method for initiating each new finger, hand,
or fist jam varies. Your two options include crossing over
or shuffling. Shuffling involves continuously using the
same hand to reach for the next jam, and using the opposite hand jammed about chest high for leverage and sta-
bilization (*Illustrations: Clockwise 1 thru 5 below*). This technique works well on cracks that lean or traverse. It is also
ideal on straight-up cracks when you need to conserve
energy and cover a long distance, but do not necessarily
have to reach high.

Fist jamming

Shuffling

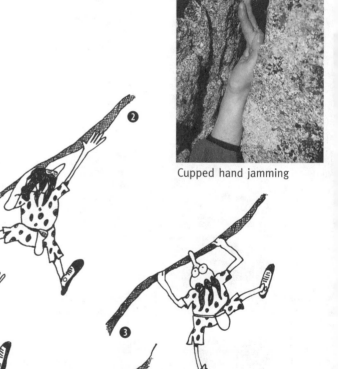

Cupped hand jamming

Hand Taping

Learning to crack climb is brutal on the hands. Skin loss and bruising can be prevented by a number of taping methods. This technique requires 1½" (3.75cm) cloth medical tape, and allows you to remove the tape from each hand in one piece to reuse it later. Unlike other methods, this technique purposely avoids taping across the palm of your hand, which is uncomfortable and unnecessary.

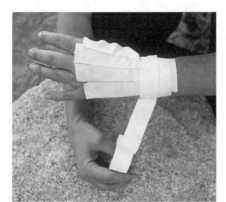

1. Adhere 3-4 individual tape strips to the back of your hand lengthwise between wrist and fingers. (For added protection, make it a double layer.)

2. Create 3-4 wraps with the tape around your wrist.

3. Beginning at the wrist, make several passages of tape up and around each finger and down across the back of the hand. After each passage, angle the tape slightly to make one wrap around the wrist. Incorporate all fingers, or eliminate the thumb or smallest finger, depending on the amount of protection desired.

Continued on next page

Taping Tips:

• With the exception of the initial wrist wraps, this process can usually be done with one or two continuous pieces of tape. For a tidier result cut tape after each wrap, but make sure you tuck all ends away securely, and anchor your work with a few wrist wraps when finishing.

• A tape job that is too tight will restrict movement and cut off blood supply. To avoid this, periodically flex your fingers and hands as you wrap, and keep your wrist wraps snug but not tight. If your skin bulges out from under the tape, it's probably too tight.

• Because all cloth medical tape isn't created equal, try several brands until you find one that works well. I recommend Johnson & Johnson's. Plastic tape is not an option—it's too flimsy and doesn't adhere. Purchase cloth tape either from either a pharmacy or a climbing retailer.

• Tincture of benzoin helps tape adhere better. Apply a thin layer to the back of your hands before taping.

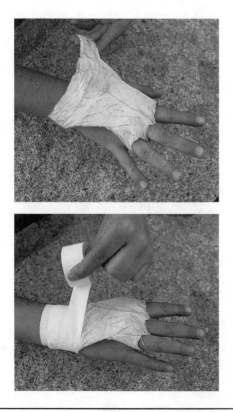

Reusing Tape

1. To remove a wrap, use scissors to clip the tape carefully on the underside of your wrist and peel/slide it off. To reuse a wrap, slide it on and add tape around the wrist to secure it. Apply tincture of benzoin for added security.

Crossing Over

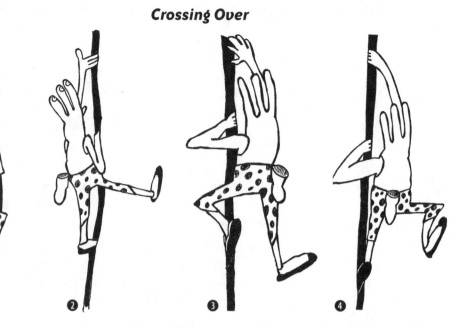

To reach higher, crossing over works better. This technique looks a little like the crawl stroke—you're going to be reaching for jams with alternating lead hands (*Illustrations: 1 thru 4 above*). Crossing over on leaning cracks, though, is not ideal because it prevents you from keeping your weight directly on your feet. With experience your body will intuitively know whether to cross over or shuffle.

Chimneys

Chimneys have a bad rap, probably because they are often difficult to protect on lead. Yet a standard, medium-width chimney can be delightful—often having protection options deep inside or along its sidewalls. Begin by wedging yourself between the chimney walls with your buttocks and back pressed up against one and your feet pressed against the other. Create resistance by exerting pressure between the palms of your hands, buttocks, back, legs, and feet. To make upward progress, alternately walk your feet and scoot your butt up, with leverage from your palms pressed against either wall. Depending on chimney architecture, either keep both feet against the front wall or place them oppositionally against both walls (*Illustrations: 1a left and 1b opposite page, top right*).

Climbing a standard chimney

As you progress, avoid placing your feet too low—keep them as high as possible for optimal security. Utilize any face holds or cracks—no matter how small—for increased friction. Don't wedge yourself so deeply in the chimney that you miss easier climbing out toward the lip (where those new to chimney technique are afraid to go). In slightly wider chimneys, keep one foot on the front wall and the other on the rear wall, bridging the gap also with the palms of your hands, as you move upward one foot at a time *(Illustration: 2, bottom right)*.

Off-width cracks, squeeze chimneys, and flares involve advanced jamming techniques not covered in this book. Nevertheless, the basic skills you cultivate today climbing standard cracks provide the foundation to master these more advanced techniques. When you've got your basic crack skills honed, check out Long and Luebben's *Advanced Rock Climbing* for tips on wide crack variants requiring advanced skills. See Steph Davis's 1998 article in *Climbing* (June 15, 1998, No. 177) for how to climb off-width thin cracks using techniques such as tight hands, ring locks, and ratchets.

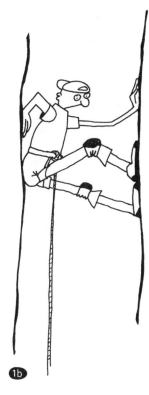

FOLLOWING & CLEANING

Mastering the skills of following and cleaning trad pitches are crucial if your sights are set on leading. Unless you can appreciate these as vital learning tools, they can be trying tasks. Your ability to follow and clean with finesse, together with your overall attitude, makes good use of your time on the rock. A positive, competent follower always has more climbing invitations than an inexperienced, fumbling and grumbling, second. When instructing new lead climbers—serious about the sport and wanting to climb as much as possible—I teach them first how to become good followers. Logging in lead climbing hours at the crags will follow. The climbers you follow before and during your initial trad leading experiences influence your abilities and style more than anyone (or anything) else. So, choose your partners carefully.

Wide chimney technique

Besides ensuring you get the most out of your experiences as follower, these tips help build the skills you need for leading.

At the Base

Make sure everything you need is within arm's reach before putting the leader on belay. Have your shoes on so you're prepared to climb. If the weather is chilly, put your fleece on before the leader begins. On the ground, always tie into the end of the rope before the leader sets off. This way, when the leader finishes the pitch and pulls the rope up, you don't risk it going too far, if you're not paying attention. Now, you're ready to climb.

Belaying

Belay as close to the base of the wall as possible, thereby preventing unnecessary outward force on the lead protection if the leader falls (see *"backward zipper"* in Chapter 5). Proper positioning also eliminates the risks of the leader falling farther (since there's less rope out) and your being slammed into the wall, if the force is significant. Maintain about an arm's length of slack rope in the system, except when the leader is near the ground or a ledge. This prevents the leader from feeling rope resistance when needing to clip a piece quickly. It might prevent your pulling the leader off a traverse, too. As the slack rope disappears, feed out more. The leader appreciates an attentive belay; your chatting with other climbers either at the base or a belay ledge can indicate otherwise.

Climbing

As the follower, notice how each piece of protection is placed. Ask yourself why the leader chose that particular piece at that specific stance. Why is there a shoulder-length runner on it instead of a quickdraw? Assess the distances between pieces and think how and why they vary. Notice how certain placements protect the leader from hitting obstacles in case of a fall. If you find a piece of protection has walked or popped out, analyze how this occurred and what could have been done to prevent it. Imagine yourself in the leader's position placing each piece: find the most energy-efficient stance, remove the piece, then reset it yourself for practice. Climb smoothly as if you were on lead; move carefully and pretend that falling is not an option (but don't dawdle). Re-rack gear neatly and orderly throughout the pitch; don't wait to reach the belay anchor to get organized. Finally, do your utmost not to whine.

At the Belay Anchor

As your partner re-racks, hand him or her one piece at a time—a quickdraw assembled with two carabiners is considered one piece, while a Stopper attached to a carabiner is two (if the leader racks Stoppers in groups). Because an SLCD without a 'biner is a half of a piece, be sure each cam has one carabiner attached. In other words offer pieces ready to clip onto the leader's rack. When you transfer more than one at a time, you both risk dropping something.

Particularly on a multipitch route, act efficiently at the belay and be as helpful as possible in preparing for the next pitch. Offer to re-flake the rope and get water out of the pack. If you're not doing anything, ask your partner what you can do. This scenario is known as the *changeover*, which is discussed in depth in Chapter 6.

Cleaning

As you remove protection, stay organized. Rack each piece individually in order of size, disassembling Stoppers on quickdraws and keeping all Stoppers on one carabiner. Not only will your partner appreciate it when exchanging gear at the belay, but climbing is easier if you're not disheveled with slings dangling down to your knees and hardware stacking up on the rope at your waist.

When approaching a piece of protection, leave it clipped to the rope. If it remains attached and you drop it, the piece will just slide down to your waist. For further security removing the piece, clip it while still attached to the rope into your sling; then unclip it from the rope.

Approach SLCD removal with finesse and delicacy, and passive pro removal with gusto. Although yanking forcefully to remove Stoppers is a common method of removal, you can save your wireds from damaging kinks if you use your nut tool. If you do choose to yank, close your mouth prior to removal to protect your pearly whites. Don't give up easily. Persistency and determination usually prevail in extracting overcammed SLCDs or stubbornly wedged Stoppers.

In summary, the ideal follower climbs swiftly, cleans the pitch with efficiency and success, stays organized, and keeps the leader safe by providing an attentive belay and feeding rope out smoothly. He or she is always prepared to climb when the rope tightens, doesn't drop gear, and doesn't whine (too much). After acquiring these skills, you shouldn't have a problem finding climbing partners, and, once you start leading, your rope-handling and gear-management skills will be that much more developed.

RAPPEL OVERVIEW

Rappelling skills are necessary for anyone venturing into traditional climbing. Most climbers learning to trad lead already have basic rappelling skills. But if you were introduced to the sport through indoor gym climbing or sport cragging, your descent experience may have been limited to being lowered by a partner.

Gear Dependence

In trad free climbing, rappelling is one of the few scenarios where you rely completely upon your equipment and anchors. During an ascent, gear and anchors play essentially the role of a safety net. Sometimes you can climb several pitches without ever weighting your harness, the rope, pieces of protection, or even the anchors. In altering your relationship with equipment, rappelling requires a leap of faith and a shift toward complete dependence. As long as climbers possess the appropriate skills and devote their complete attention to the task, rappelling can be relatively safe, but keep in mind that a small mistake can be fatal.

Inexperienced rappellers should practice once or twice with an experienced guide or mentor in a controlled setting prior to rappelling on their own. Although

Stubborn Gear Removal Tips

Stoppers

• To dislodge a Stopper welded into place, tap with a carabiner or a rock on the bottom of your nut tool placed against the underside of the Stopper.

• The hook on your nut tool is invaluable for leveraging out larger Stoppers with eyeholes *(Photo: above)*.

• Besides the use of your nut tool, don't underestimate the results of some finger maneuvering, especially on Stoppers that are partially loose.

• Look for wider sections above or below Stopper placements that indicate how a piece was slotted; reverse that action to retrieve it. Better yet, if you can hear your partner, ask him or her (likewise for difficult-to-remove SLCDs).

SLCDs

• Smaller SLCDs are often more difficult to extract because of their minimal camming range. If you're unable to extract a small cam on your first try, try gently rocking the stem while retracting the trigger as tightly as possible and pulling outward.

• For an SLCD that has walked so deeply into a crack you cannot reach it, use the hook on your nut tool and the loop on the end of a Stopper to retract its trigger bar.

• Use the hook on your nut tool to retract individually inverted cams on larger SLCDs without cam stops.

Left belayer clipped in with a cow's tail; right belayer uses a daisy chain.

elementary descriptions of how to rappel are not included in this text, a basic overview is. Tips are intended to supplement the newcomer's sessions with a mentor or a guide, and provide those with more experience reinforcement of several crucial concepts. Explanations assume climbers are clipped in safely at a reliable anchor with a locking carabiner and either a *cow's tail* (a sling that has been girth-hitched to your rappel/belay loop) or a *daisy chain* (specialty webbing with several sewn loops designed for adjustable clip-ins) *(Photo: left)*.

The Rope(s)

Rappels are done on one rope or on two tied together. Before getting on any route with a rappel descent, determine the length of each rappel. To descend distances less than half the length of your rope, a single rope doubled at its center is sufficient. For longer rappels, use two ropes. If you're unsure of a rappel's length, bring a second rope. Two ropes of similar diameter can be tied together for double-rope rappels by one of several knots. I recommend either the double fisherman's (grapevine) or the *flat overhand* (see Chapter 8). Use a triple fisherman's when connecting dissimilar diameter ropes. Because of the knot, only one rope can be pulled to retrieve your lines from below; note which one before heading down.

Avoiding Fatal Mistakes

Deadly rappel errors can result when a climber rappels off the ends of either two equal-length rope strands *(Illustration: left)* or two uneven strands *(Illustration: opposite page, top)*. If you accidently rappel on uneven lines and the shorter strand's end passes through the rappel device, your weight suddenly shifts onto the longer strand and the rope(s) are pulled through the anchor. Avoid these mistakes by taking some simple precautions. First, tie secure individual "stopper" knots *(Photos: 1 and 2 below)* on the ends of each strand before tossing your rope(s) down the line of descent. (Note: If the rappel is a "rope-stretcher"—if it requires every inch to reach the ground or next anchor—skip the stopper knots but be sure to use a brake-line backup.) After tossing each rope off separately (to avoid potential tangles), verify that each free end reaches the ground (or the next anchor). Don't accept ropes that are tangled midway or have landed short. Pull these lines up and take the time to toss them again. For added security, especially on descents where the ground or next anchor is not visible, clip a carabiner through each knot. Finally, before initiating the rappel, confirm that the center of your rope is at anchor level. (Bicolored and bipatterned ropes make identifying a rope's midpoint easy. But don't become complacent—an experienced and very competent fellow guide once rappelled off an uneven bicolored rope.)

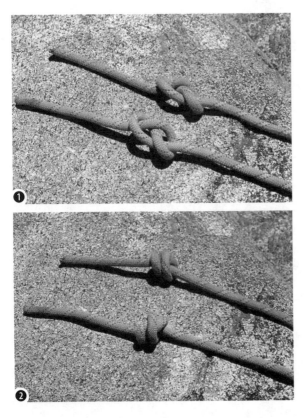

Tying a "stopper" knot to the free end of each rappel line may prevent rappelling off the end of your rope(s). Effective "stopper" knots include the single figure eight (1); and half of a double fisherman's (2).

Friction hitch used to create a backup brake (1). The safety feature activated (2).

Brake-Line Backup

To create a backup brake mechanism, attach a friction hitch with one short loop (approximately 1' or 30 cm) of 6 mm of nylon cord onto both of your brake lines below your device. (To prepare a loop for this purpose, purchase at least 2' (60 cm) of cord in order have enough for knot and tails; trim as needed.) Clip it to your leg loop with a carabiner, and keep it loose with your brake hand on or slightly above it as you descend *(Photo: 1 left)*. Most climbers I know prefer using the *autoblock* (see Chapter 8) for this purpose. Some climbers prefer to attach their backup above their rappel device. If you prefer this method, clip the friction hitch to your harness at your waist and tend it carefully on the descent to prevent it from getting sucked into the device.

In the event you are hit by rockfall or pass out and lose control, the friction hitch will tighten *(Photo: 2 left)* and prevent you from plummeting downward. The friction-hitch backup is a must for climbers rappelling with a heavy pack, and is a good idea for exhausted climbers facing multiple rappels. Before descending, though, make sure the cord is short enough to avoid getting sucked into your rappel device. To prevent any likelihood that this could happen, you can extend your braking device by adding a sling or quickdraw to your harness rappel loop as shown in photos 1 and 2. Although your device is now farther away from you, the braking capabilities remain the same. This is common practice by European guides when descending with novice rappellers. Not only does it keep the braking device safely away from the backup friction hitch, it also keeps it away from loose clothing or hair.

Safety Check

Before you unclip from the anchors for any rappel descent, mentally review the following checklist:

✓ Are the anchor, slings, and masterpoint reliable? Are recently tied newer slings knotted tightly with adequate tails?

✓ Is my carabiner locked?

✓ Is the rope fed properly through my rappel device and locker?

✓ Is my harness doubled back?

✓ Are my hair and/-or loose clothing secured away from the device? (Getting hair caught in your device on rappel is extremely dangerous and, among other complications, can result in serious scalp injuries. Though easily prevented, it is surprisingly common.)

✓ Is the center of the rope running through the masterpoint? Are the two rappel strands equal?

✓ Are the ropes tangle-free? Do they reach the ground or the next rappel station?

✓ If rope length is adequate to reach the next anchor or the ground, did I tie knots in each rope end?

✓ Is my backup hitch tied and attached correctly? Is it short enough to not get sucked into my device?

✓ On a double-rope rappel, is the knot secure and tied correctly? Which rope will I pull to retrieve the lines from below?

✓ Are the ropes running across any sharp terrain? If necessary, use slings to extend your masterpoint *(Illustrations: 1 and 2 above)* or pad the sharp area with duct tape or clothing.

Use slings to extend your masterpoint if the rappel rope is subject to a sharp edge.

Rope Retrieval Tips

You risk rappel ropes getting stuck upon every retrieval. Since even the finest climbing day will be tainted by the ugly experience of dealing with a stuck rope, here are some tips to avoid it:

• After the first partner rappels, ask him or her to test pull the rope. If it appears the knot might get stuck on something within the first several feet of the anchor (which is usually the problem area), consider moving the knot below the suspect section and begin your rappel below it *(Illustration: right)*. Use extreme care as you begin the rappel, as you may have to downclimb a short distance while holding onto your brake-line. Do not attempt this if the rope is barely long enough to complete a full-length rappel as the ends will be uneven.

• If you're the last person to rappel, maintain control of the rope ends after removing your device to keep them from twisting upon your release. Before pulling your lines, be sure they're free of any twists or knots.

• When rappelling on two ropes of differing diameters in windy conditions, arrange the knot so that you can pull the thinner rope during retrieval. Gusts are less likely to sweep the heftier rope into a nearby obstacle.

• On a single-rope rappel, you can choose to pull either end of the rope. Examine the rock and surrounding terrain to determine which side has less snag possibilities and pull from that side. For instance, if a tree is growing out of a crack halfway up the right side of the wall, opt to pull the left end.

Continued on next page

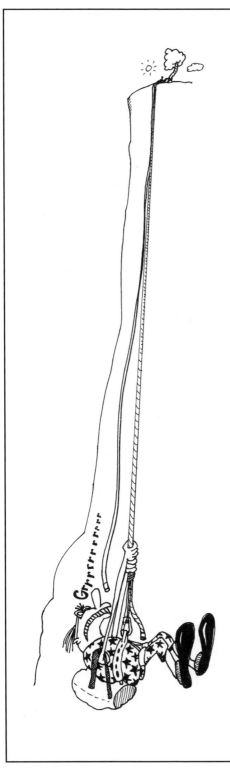

- If you feel tension when retrieving the rope, try flipping it out of a potential snag, and possibly prevent it from wedging in even tighter.

- Sometimes during retrieval, the knot of your rappel lines gets hung up on a lip. If you suspect this is the case with your ropes, have your partner hold onto the rope leading to the knot, then grab the other non-knotted side. With a firm whip of the rope, send a vertical wave up toward the anchor. Moments after—when the swell reaches the snag—have your partner pull the other end. The wave motion may create enough force to lift the knot from the rock, and, with the other end pulled, to free the rope.

- If your final resort is brute strength, make the most of your effort by attaching yourself to the stubborn side of the rope via a friction hitch to achieve maximum torque ability *(Illustration: left)*.

- In any difficult retrieval situation, prepare to take cover if loose rock is dislodged.

- Never try to retrieve ropes from a web of wet slings; the friction is tremendous. Sacrifice a couple carabiners from your rack; the replacement cost is minor compared to the grief avoided. Remember to reverse and oppose the gates.

Building the basic skill foundation a traditional leader needs takes time and patience. You must be confident and comfortable placing reliable gear, building solid anchors, tackling moderate cracks, and descending via rappelling to move on to the next learning phase. Mastering these skills can only occur with a lot of practice, and feedback from experts. As you gain experience in low-risk settings, scout for short routes with modest ratings that can be top-roped; there, you will eventually combine these skills with additional techniques described in Chapter 5, "The Single-Pitch Trad Lead."

Chapter 5

The Single-Pitch Trad Lead

For your first trad lead, choose a single-pitch route offering ample protection opportunities with good stances for resting and placing gear. The climb is ideally one you have previously followed or top-roped successfully. Choose a route of moderate difficulty so that the physical climb can be secondary in focus to gear placement and rope management—a few ratings below the level of ability at which you can easily follow is optimal. For example, if you've managed to eke up a few 5.9 top-ropes but feel completely solid following 5.7-5.8, then start on a 5.6 lead.

If your experience on traditional routes is minimal and your experience with ratings has been limited to those of sport routes, consider that you're no longer on common ground. The sport climber shifting to trad climber initially finds that ratings rarely seem equally transferable (see Chapter 9). Pick something a little more moderate to ensure that your transition is gentle, and then advance to more difficult routes at a modest pace.

Bill McChesney

Lisa Hathaway

Climber: Noah Bigwood
Years Trad Free Climbing: 23
Average Trad Lead Ability: Up to 5.13 (on-sight)
Favorite Trad Climbing Area(s): Canyonlands (Southern Utah)
Most Respected Trad Free Climber: Kennan Harvey (and anyone
     who gives each pitch their undivided attention and then is
     happy and humble about the outcome)

Surviving the Learning Curve

Because they require you hold your ambitions in check while maintaining self-confidence, beginnings are delicate times. In learning to lead traditional climbs you face challenges and make decisions with your life (and often that of your partner) on the line. Because all climbing routes introduce different challenges, each climber must assess his or her own strengths and weaknesses, and reach beyond fear to gain confidence. Yet, some basic principles can help you survive the learning curve and emerge a safer, stronger, and more confident leader.

Know Your Limit—Everyone is limited by something: some confront fears, others struggle with gear and knots, nearly all get pumped, and everyone has a physical limit to how hard they can climb. If you've spent some time bouldering, top-roping, and following others, you have a good idea where your limitations lie. Not to say you shouldn't be pushing yourself; in order to progress you'll have to move out of your comfort zone. Yet, good leaders look for challenges they can surmount and grow from, not ones that will shut them down.

Continued on next page

Climb Carefully—The sheer excitement of climbing makes you hurry and feel rushed—slow down! Take time to do everything right the first time and then double-check it. Hurrying results in mistakes (especially when learning) and mistakes, if they don't kill you, will slow you down. Whatever has you hurrying, if you start making mistakes, can spiral out of control. Enjoy the journey as well as the destination by taking your time.

Savor Every Lead—Though when scared and pushing your limits climbing can feel more burdensome than pleasurable, accept both burdens and glory in the mantle of a traditional lead climber. To lead a route, step up to the rock with anticipation and confidence, not angst and dread. If you are not having fun, or simply not looking forward to every lead (whether you're nervous or not), take a step back. Regain your comfort level to rediscover the fun. When you're having fun you climb better, learn more, and build confidence. Savor the experience of every lead.

—Noah Bigwood

LEADING ON TOP-ROPE

Lead climbing with a backup top-rope lets you assimilate the tools you've learned on the ground and work out the kinks of your system in a relatively safe setting. The stakes are lower with the security of a top-rope, so you can focus on technical tasks without agonizing over the consequences of falling. To accommodate a top-rope, the chosen routes must be half the length of your rope.

Expert Feedback

Ask your mentor to coach you and critique your performance. If you don't have one, be certain your partner has enough trad leading experience to analyze your lead discerningly, examine gear placements, and coach you along as needed. Without an expert's feedback you may not be able to recognize a mistake. Take your time, ask for advice, and iron out the wrinkles in your technique before you consider eliminating the safety net of the top-rope. If you find yourself falling with frequency or avoiding gear placements because of awkward or strenuous stances, work on a less challenging route. Continue top-roping your leads until you can successfully coordinate their physical and mental demands with relative comfort and ease.

The Setup

You need two ropes for a simulated lead—one for your top-rope and the other for your lead rope. Set up a top-rope anchor, tie into one end of the top-rope, and have your partner put you on belay. Next, carefully uncoil your lead rope at the base so that it will feed out neatly, and tie into it. You are tied into both ropes but your partner need only belay you on the top-rope line. Protect any significant traverses with a pre-placed directional to prevent a potential swinging fall.

AT THE BASE

Racking Up

Every seasoned climber has developed a method of racking gear that best suits his/her physique and personal preferences. Most gear leaders use a combination of racking methods that utilize their harness loops, as well as a gear sling. On short routes some climbers rack solely on their harness loops. Longer routes often require the additional use of a gear sling. Whatever the case, as a new leader, assembling your rack consistently the same way on every lead lets you expedite gear selection and reduce the fumble factor.

Though consistency is your watchword, still remain open to change. Because the rack is shared in multipitch climbing, it requires racking diversity. Yet without some overlap, precious time is lost at belays (see Chapter 6). On the single pitch front flexibility is beneficial, too. For instance, if you've got a chimney to tackle, wearing gear on you harness loops—increasing friction against your hindquarters—can impede your progress. Or the route might dictate switching the gear sling from one shoulder to the other. An example is a crack that leans significantly to the right. In this scenario, if the rack is slung over your right shoulder, your gear will alternately be in the way (annoying) or completely out of view (unreachable). Whatever the case, be prepared to alter your primary racking system to accommodate the pitch. Get into the habit of scoping out the upcoming pitch and adjusting your rack accordingly before casting off.

Examine the route description and topo in your guidebook, and then view the route itself to determine which pieces you're likely to need. Even if the topo indicates "pro to 3 inches (7.5cm)," don't be surprised if the opportunity to place something larger arises. If the topo doesn't indicate sizes, and/or you can't get a visual of the entire route, take a couple pieces of each size up to 4" (10cm) and, if you have one, bring a 5" (12.5cm) piece just to be safe. If you're new to trad climbing, contending with wide cracks is going to be difficult until you gain more experience. So if there's *any* chance the route contains a wide section, bring appropriate-sized pieces, even if you have to borrow gear. New trad leaders commonly flail on wide sections because they underestimated the severity of, say, a 5.8 wide crack—very different from a 5.8-face or a 5.8-hand crack. And, chances are, they aren't carrying the appropriate-sized gear for protection. It's safer to over- rather than underestimate the amount of gear you'll need during your first few years on trad terrain, particularly when it comes to wide gear. Going light is often desirable but not while you're learning.

Rack your SLCDs according to size, each with its own single carabiner. I find that pieces are most easily removed if the carabiner gate is clipped facing my body, but know a few longtime climbers that prefer the gates facing outward. On the gear sling, I keep the smallest cams closest to my navel and the largest cams toward my hip. Others may choose the opposite, but I find that bulkier pieces ride more comfortably the farther they are from my groin. Such details are personal choices and make no difference in the single-pitch arena.

You may choose to color code like-sized SLCDs with similar colored webbing. SLCD sling colors (and in some cases anodized cam colors) for specific sizes from some manufacturers already correspond with other brands, but many do not and cannot because actual sizes differ too much. If you choose to color code cams, you have to remove the manufacturer's sewn runner on some pieces and replace them with your own hand-tied webbing. (Some suppliers offer sewn sling replacement for SLCDs, but webbing colors might be limited.) Eventually you come to associate a specific crack size with a color. I did this for several years and it definitely facilitated finding the right piece pronto. The drawback of color coding becomes apparent when you use someone else's gear (vice versa when another climber uses yours). You'll assess the crack size, then reach down for "yellow." What you find isn't always what you expect.

Rack a standard trad Stopper selection generally on two to three carabiners, preferably ovals where space is more plentiful. Too many nuts on one carabiner increases the risk of dropping them when you're rifling through your selection on lead. Two schools exist regarding the racking of nuts. Some leaders carry their micro to small nuts on one carabiner, and medium to large nuts on one or two others. Some carry a mix of sizes on each carabiner, so that if the unfortunate occasion arises that you drop one of the 'biners, you still have a decent range of nuts remaining to get you off the climb. The Stopper selection you bring might be recommended by the local guidebook. Otherwise, I suggest a full set with doubles in the ¼-½"(6-12mm) range.

Hexes and Tri-Cams can either be racked separately or in groups. If you have few or no SLCDs, rack each on its own 'biner for quick and easy placement on lead. If Hexes and Tri-Cams supplement your standard rack, it might be easier to group several on an oval carabiner.

The total number of quickdraws, runners, and carabiners you'll need depends upon your route length and anticipated traversing. The most versatile quickdraw is a tripled 22-24" (50-60cm) runner with a carabiner at each end (see Chapter 3). Unlike the shorter sewn quickdraws, these can be unraveled and used as longer runners. Carry most of your slings as quickdraws on straight-up, direct routes. On routes that wander and traverse, carry them as open shoulder-length slings over your head and across the opposite shoulder from the rack. Because you'll most likely also need a 'biner when you need a runner, rack each with a single carabiner. For quick and easy removal, make sure you put these on *after* you put on the rack. Double-length (44" or 110cm) runners serve you well on meandering terrain, so bring at least one of these on indirect routes.

The majority of your remaining carabiners are considered "free" or "single" ones. When deciding how many free 'biners to bring on a single pitch, consider that a cordelette belay anchor requires anywhere from three to six. So in addition to the carabiners attached to runners and quickdraws, plan on carrying at least six single ones, and maybe a few more for unforeseen circumstances. Some climbers carry free 'biners tripled or in pairs. Others prefer linking them together in a chain of five, clipping the middle 'biner to a harness loop.

If on lead you forget a crucial piece of gear in your pack on the ground, you can have your belayer send it up, provided you've got anchoring options and used less than half your rope's length. Set up a quick anchor, clip in, and pull up a loop of slack that can be lowered to the belayer to which the piece(s) can be clipped and raised. And although it's easier for your belayer to feed out slack by taking you off belay, ask that the belayer complete the task while keeping you on belay.

The Base Belay

At the base you must determine whether or not to establish an anchor for your belayer. To decide first consider your location. If the route starts from a small pedestal or outcropping, you need a base anchor that incorporates a piece that can withstand a downward force. This safeguards you (and your partner) from tumbling off the stance should you rip out all of your pieces on lead, or fall prior to placing your first piece (*Illustration: page 107*). If the pitch begins from flat ground there's little need for an anchor. However, if you weigh significantly more than your belayer, an anchor that can withstand an upward force and prevent your fall force from lifting the belayer off the ground might be appreciated. If your belayer is not anchored and does get pulled up, you're going to fall that much farther. Still, this scenario allows the movement of the belayer's body to absorb some of the force generated in the fall, placing less impact on other parts of the system. If the route is notorious for tricky placements and/or lots of smaller

The Harness Ensemble

Each climber's harness ensemble should include the following:

• Large locking carabiner and belay/rappel device;

• Another locking carabiner for clipping into anchors;

• Cordelette or Web-o-lette™ for setting pre-equalized anchors;

• Nut tool; and

• Approximately 2' (60cm) of 6mm nylon accessory cord tied in a loop for use as a rappel backup (see Chapter 4).

Optional:

• Self-rescue tools (see Chapter 7)—strongly recommended, especially on long, multipitch routes;

• A small knife for removing old webbing from belay/rappel stations;

• Two rappel rings or sacrificial carabiners to augment a scrawny or antiquated rappel station (see Chapter 6); and

• A daisy chain for rappel-anchor clip-ins (a girthed runner also works).

placements, you may want to forgo the anchor. Just make sure the belayer knows that he or she is being used as a fall-force reducer.

Many trad climbers, myself included, prefer to skip the initial (base) belay anchor when routes begin from the ground. Besides the benefit of utilizing the belayer as a force-reducer, he or she can duck out of the way of potential rockfall. If you are concerned about a weight discrepancy, situate your belayer in a stable and secure position wedged between two features (trees, boulders, etc.) at the base of the climb. If this isn't possible, have the belayer brace one leg against the wall to act as a shock absorber.

If you are utilizing an anchor, have your belayer clip into the anchor point with the rope after tying in. The benefits of using the rope versus a sling are that:

1. You don't have to dedicate a sling to this task;

2. Your belayer is tied into the rope end and ready to climb; and

3. The rope used as a leash—something you can't do with a sling (unless you tie several together, creating a sling shortage on lead)—allows the belayer to stand at the base if the anchor is a distance away.

Should have established an anchor . . .

A clove hitch or *figure-eight on a bight* is equally appropriate for this purpose. I prefer a clove hitch because it is easily adjusted, although the figure-eight is slightly stronger. As long as the clove hitch is tightened after knotting and the load is on the appropriate strand (see Chapter 8), it is perfectly suitable.

PING!!

Improper belayer positioning can create unwanted lateral forces on lead protection

As discussed briefly in Chapter 4, your belayer should be positioned directly below the first protectable moves of the pitch, and as close to the wall as possible. If he or she belays away from the wall and a lead fall occurs, the taut rope will create unwanted lateral force on your protection. *(Illustration: left)* Depending on the anticipated load direction of your first lead placement, it could rip out. In addition, an unanchored belayer far from the wall could be slammed against the rock if the fall force is great, and sudden slack in the system could result in a longer fall for the lead climber.

If your first piece cannot withstand an upward and/or lateral force and it fails, the torque may shift to the next highest piece, ripping it out, too. As momentum builds and each of your remaining pieces experiences force, it becomes possible that they all may fail. This hazardous scenario is known as a backward zipper. (See page 113 for other potential backward-zipper scenarios).

Safety Check

After failing to complete her tie-in knot on a toprope, several years ago world-class climber Lynn Hill leaned back to be lowered by her belayer and suffered a near ground fall. This was the first time I recall my partner's suggesting we check each other's knots and harnesses. News traveled fast and, before long, most climbers I know began doing safety checks before leaving the ground. No matter how often you climb or how hard you crank, you're not exempt from making a simple mistake. Why? Because you're human (although I sometimes wonder about Hill). Check each other's knots and buckles *every time* you leave the ground. Don't be embarrassed to check and don't be insulted when checked. If this warps your ego, take up a sport with fewer risks.

COMMUNICATION

When communicating with your partner on a climb, don't compete with the buzz of planes overhead, the roar of cars passing below, and other climbers hollering commands within the vicinity. Whenever possible, wait for a moment of silence, then give the command. When wind, rushing water, or other natural audio phenomena could impede communication, face your partner and belt out your command.

Use your partner's name with each command. Essential when other climbing parties are nearby, this heightens your partner's awareness of the communication. Don't trust your ability to differentiate your partner's voice from those of the lads cranking up a route around the corner. If you're on a dicey runout pulling some hard moves and your partner responds to another climber's request for "slack"—after your flash flood of terror subsides and the rope is adjusted—you appreciate the value in using names with commands.

Verbal Commands

With each new partner agree on which communication terms to use. The following are basic commands used predominately in the US:

On Belay—With the rope leading to the climber secured into the belay device, the belayer signals his/her readiness for the climber to begin.

Climbing—The climber reports that he/she is beginning.

Climb On—The belayer affirms a readiness for the climber to begin.

Slack—The climber requests some slack in the rope—unless otherwise specified about an arm's length. Common reasons for slack include the climber's: needing the rope tension lessened to more effectively clean a piece of protection, needing slack to down-climb if he/she has gone *off-route*, wanting to rest at a lower stance, and, wanting to try again after having botched a sequence. A climber might also request slack when preparing to follow a traverse where rope tension could hinder balance.

Tension/Take—The climber signals the belayer to take in any extra slack and lock off the belay device so he/she can hang on the rope.

Up-rope—The climber cues the belayer to pay closer attention and take in extra slack. As the climber, avoid the common mistake of requesting your belayer "Take up the slack." What the belayer might hear is just the word "Slack," and the result is obvious—a real bummer!

Watch Me—The climber indicates a difficult move ahead and requests increased alertness from the belayer.

Falling—The climber alerts the belayer to take in slack and prepare to lock off the belay device.

Rock!—Not limited to rocks, use this command for all falling objects, whether it be a piece of gear, a camera, a water bottle, a sheet of ice, your helmet, a tiny pebble, a clod of dirt, or whatever else you lugged up.

Off Belay—The leader communicates to the belayer his/her no longer needing belay-system security, having clipped into an established anchor. If the belayer is *absolutely* certain this was the command given, he/she may disengage the belay device. (Climbers from other English-speaking countries might shout "Safe" instead.)

Belay Off—The belayer alerts the climber that the device is disengaged and the belay done. By shouting "Belay off" you acknowledge the leader is indeed clipped to an anchor and no longer needs the security of the belay. If there was any miscommunication and the climber is *not* clipped securely, this gives him/her the opportunity to respond. For this reason, I like to shout this command seconds *before* disengaging my device— just in case. "Belay off" also tells the leader to pull up the rope to prepare the belay system that will eventually protect the follower. If you fail to affirm that the belay's off, the leader wastes precious time instead of moving on to the next task.

Avoid extra words whenever possible; by using basic commands you decrease the chance of miscommunication. If you say more, don't plan on being understood. I had a partner who liked to say "Gimme some" instead of "Slack." In response to "Slack" I'm like Pavlov's dog; the rope feeds through my device immediately without much thought. But hearing anything else, I need several seconds to process, interpret, and verify it. This wastes time and can result in further miscommunication.

Backup Tactile Commands

If there's a possibility that you won't be able to hear your partner once you've reached the belay anchor, discuss a backup plan for tactile communication. Three firm tugs can translate to "On belay." Although not optimal, this is better than no plan at all. Alternately, partners could agree prior to the ascent that when the rope tightens, the leader has set up an anchor and engaged the belay. In this scenario the leader mustn't pull the rope up until the anchor is fixed and he/she ready to belay. The second keeps the leader on belay until the rope tightens. All commands are still shouted. If you're the follower climbing, you can be fairly certain that you're on belay if the rope is pulled tight with each move you make. The scenario where the leader accidentally climbs past the designated belay, and tugs the rope in attempting to move higher, unaware that there is no more rope left, is the obvious glitch in both of these plans. The same problem ensues if the pitch is a full rope length. Because these choices involve a lot of risk, they should only be used as last resorts.

Two-Way Radios

Once while I was instructing a beginning climbing class, the students were watching two men using two-way radios on a nearby route that is notorious for communication difficulties. Having traveled around a corner and over a roof, the leader was out of his belayer's sight. Each time he set a placement, he spoke to his belayer over the radio. One student asked what I thought of the system. Preferring not to criticize the climbers as fervently as I would if I were talking to a friend, I held my tongue and, instead, asked what the students thought. Everyone agreed the system seemed ideal, but the students sensed that there must be a drawback.

From our vantage point we could see both climbers, and hear them both fairly well. The climber now at the belay was setting an anchor. He keyed his radio and we heard him tell his partner he was off belay. As he pulled the rope up, the belayer continued to sit there, feeding rope through his device, obviously unaware that the leader was off. When the rope tightened, the belayer seemed perplexed; he asked the leader through the radio if he was off but didn't receive a response. The follower sat and waited, occasionally talking into the radio but never receiving a response. By the time both realized the radios had failed, they began yelling furiously in long sentences without much volume or projection. Barely audible even to us, most of their words were lost in the wind.

With so much confusion, when the second climber finally realized he was on belay and began moving up the rock, the upper climber—adjusting his rope to move to a spot where he could lean out and see his partner—had taken him off belay. At that point we intervened, hollering frantically to the second to stay put, that he wasn't on belay anymore. Though my initial response to radio use was confirmed, the lesson unfolded in a way that my students could make up their own minds. We all agreed that reliance on radios prevented the climbers from having to be strong communicators and, when the system failed, they didn't have fully developed skills to fall back on. Radios are a personal choice but they are fallible. If you use them, keep your communication skills sharp by not relying on technology all of the time.

LEAD PROTECTION

Placing protection takes on a whole new meaning on lead. As the leader, you must learn to identify good placements for your pieces, and remain stable and focused enough to set, runner, and clip each piece correctly before moving on. To constantly shift between the physicality of climbing and the mental task of placing gear is a tremendous challenge.

Runner Usage

Your protection is only useful if it remains stationary after placement. If the rope zigzags from one piece to the next, oblique forces can tweak pieces and sometimes pull them out. The use of runners and quickdraws helps keep your gear in place by keeping the line of the rope running plumb between you and your belayer. It also prevents *rope drag* that makes it difficult (and sometimes impossible) for you to move easily on lead without feeling an unnecessary amount of tension on the rope.

To determine whether to sling your piece short or long, first consider your potential fall distance. If you use a long runner instead of a quickdraw, you're obviously going to fall that much farther. Unless you're facing a fall onto a ledge, into a dihedral, or to the ground, a few inches won't matter with a bomber piece. Next, consider the degree to which the rope could potentially zigzag, and the piece's innate susceptibility to movement. For extra security I put shoulder-length runners on all pieces with rigid stems, even when the rope is running plumb between the belayer and myself. It doesn't take much rope movement to dislodge a wired Stopper or encourage a forged Friend to walk. On the other hand, a bendable shaft SLCD with its pre-sewn sling probably doesn't need an added runner on straight-up direct stretches, when the rope runs plumb between partners. Conserve your runners for use on meandering terrain and at the belay, or you'll run out long before the pitch ends.

Multidirectional Placements

Set gear that will withstand both lateral and downward forces when runnering efforts and/or belayer positioning cannot keep the rope plumb between you and your belayer. A multidirectional placement (see Chapter 4) may be required in situations that leave you vulnerable to the dreaded backward zipper. Two obvious examples include the first piece placed preceding a traverse anywhere on a climb, and the first piece placed on any pitch when your belayer is not directly below you.

What To Runner?

Make wise decisions about how and what to runner by always looking ahead. Clues that your pro needs to be runnered with long slings include:

• You're placing a piece in a significantly deep crack or corner (not illustrated)

Continued on next page

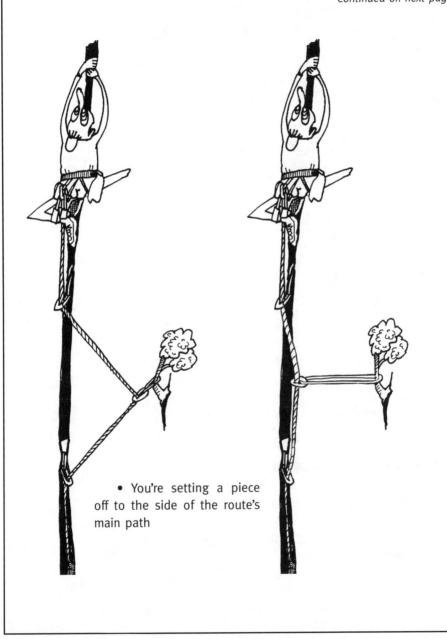

• You're setting a piece off to the side of the route's main path

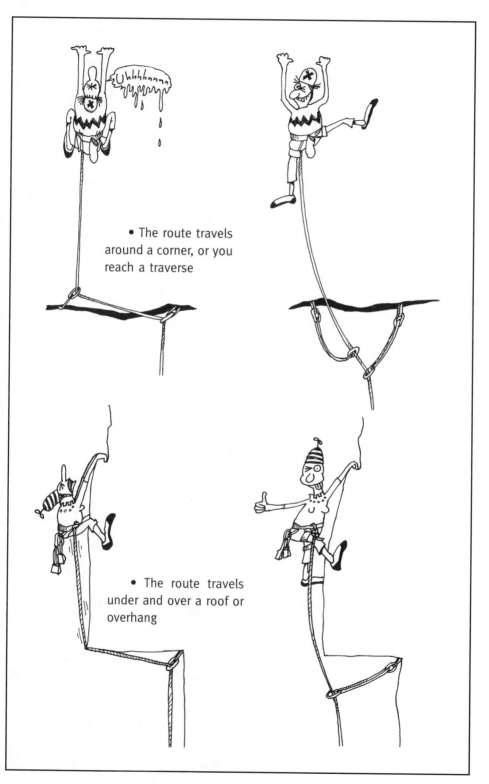

• The route travels around a corner, or you reach a traverse

• The route travels under and over a roof or overhang

Piece Selection

When choosing a piece to place on lead, consider two factors: the potential need for that particular piece higher on the pitch, and the potential force factor in relation to that piece's holding power. Should a fall occur, the amount of force each lead placement must withstand depends on how the energy generated by the fall is disbursed throughout the system. The rope absorbs energy, as does each individual piece. So, lower on a pitch, when less rope is in use and fewer pieces have been placed, your piece must withstand more force than if it were placed higher up. How do these factors affect what pieces you place and where? Some pieces have superior holding power than others. Reserve your tiny pieces and 3-cam units for placements higher up on the route. Back up each piece you identify as marginal early in the pitch with another. Also, place protection often early in the pitch (see "Placement Frequency" below).

Depending on your gear selection, you may need to conserve pieces of a certain size for use up higher. Eyeballing the route from below and checking the guidebook might give you a clue. If not, avoid complete depletion of one size or another early on the pitch. The belay anchor must also be considered. Try to reserve a few differing sizes to create a belay, unless you're certain a bolted anchor awaits.

Placement Frequency

As a climber new to gear-leading, place protection frequently, particularly during the first 25 feet of the route to reduce the load of a potential fall. Loads in relation to fall-severity ratings *(fall factors)* are detailed in a subsequent section on falling. If, purely from a fall-factor perspective, you established the optimal number of placements, the size of your required rack would anchor you to the ground. However, climber and metallurgist Steve Paterson from Los Gatos, California, has created a formula based on physics equations you can follow to keep potential fall factors reasonably low. His data suggests that if you place protection approximately every 5' (1.5m) for the first 25' (7.5m), then every 10-20' (3-6m) for the remainder of the pitch, you can significantly minimize forces, assuming each piece is placed and runnered correctly. This requires approximately one to two dozen pieces per pitch. (This guideline should not prevent you from placing additional pieces to protect *cruxes*—difficult moves—and potential ground/ledge falls.)

Paterson recommends that new trad leaders follow this formula during their first 10,000 feet of gear-leading. "That really only amounts to several single-pitch routes and a handful of long free climbs in Yosemite Valley," says Paterson, AMGA-certified top-rope guide and trad climber of nearly 30 years. By the end of your apprenticeship you will have led around 100 pitches and placed about 1,000 pieces of protection. With this experience you'll have the foundation to make your own judgments regarding when to place gear and when to *run it out*. Says Paterson, "During this time, climb routes well within your limits, and occasionally practice placing pro in spots that tax your static climbing and placement skills. Put in your mileage."

Stances

You place gear better when relaxed, so always look ahead for good stances from which to place protection. If possible, identify such locations before heading up, and plan your protection strategy accordingly. If there are few, have ready on the front of your rack the pieces you anticipate needing most. Don't stop in the middle of a crux to place gear unless absolutely necessary. Save your nuts for placement from good stances, and use SLCDs for more difficult sections, since they are generally easier and faster to place. Try to avoid clogging up a perfect finger lock or hand jam, although this may be impossible.

When I was learning, I was taught to place each piece as high as I could from each stance. Although I generally still do this for the first piece off the ground or a ledge, today I place most of my mid-lead pieces somewhere between neck and head high. The energy I save from not having to lift the rope so high is worth the few inches, and my shorter partners curse me less when cleaning.

If you are placing your first piece off the ground or off a ledge, consider bouldering up to place a high piece. Clip it and return to the stance or ground to rest before moving on. Or, if the section is particularly tricky, rest and then climb up past that piece to place another, before down-climbing back to the stance again to rest up for harder moves. You've essentially created a top-rope to protect yourself on the first few moves of a difficult section. And having conserved energy, you might be able to climb smoothly and swiftly through the bottom section of the crux, building momentum and saving strength for higher up. This technique gives you the psychological and physical strength to place your next piece from a difficult stance or, possibly, climb through the hardest section without having to stop and place a piece (provided your lower ones can protect you from a dangerous fall).

Double Placements

Place two pieces in the following instances: if the section ahead looks difficult to protect or could be a runout, if a piece is dicey, or if it provides necessary protection from a dangerous fall. Such situations might also warrant the use of a small locking 'biner and/or a *load-limiter* quickdraw (like a *Yates' Screamer*). Even when conditions are relatively safe ahead and your gear is solid, placing two pieces prior to the crux might give you the psychological boost to crank through the moves without hesitation.

Blind Placements

Never place gear blindly—you want to see your piece to determine its integrity. If this is not possible, test the piece with several meaningful yanks. Then place a second piece (if you can) and climb through the section with extreme care.

Fixed Gear

Clipping into any fixed gear is a gamble. While pitons offer temptingly quick and convenient protection (and anchor) options, many are so old that their strength is suspect—particularly if the eye of a piton is cracked. Any piton that protrudes more than ⅜" from the crack should be tied-off with a short webbing sling using a girth hitch. Back up any such placement whenever possible. Other fixed gear you might find include pieces that have gotten stuck left by other climbers. Assess the placement quality for each, as well the condition of the

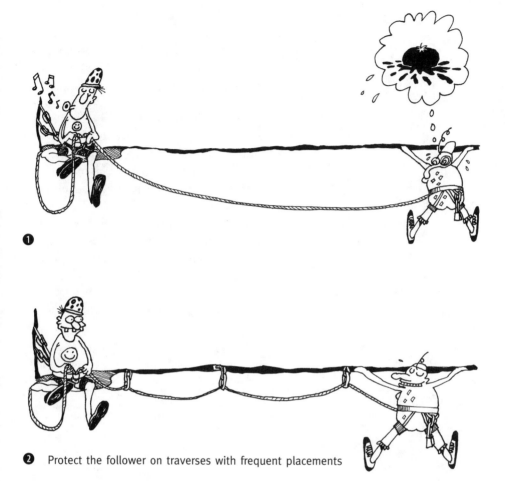

❶

❷ Protect the follower on traverses with frequent placements

webbing (if it has any), before clipping it. Whenever possible, use your own runner on such pieces. Ultimately, backing them up with additional pieces best assures your safety.

Sometimes when you're leading, a piece you're trying to manipulate into a crack becomes stuck in a useless position. If this occurs and you're experiencing difficulty removing it, let the belayer extract it (if you can afford to forfeit the piece for the remainder of the pitch). The follower, with the security of a top-rope, can expend more energy getting the wedged piece out. Don't be tempted to clip a poorly established piece unless you're certain it's stable; it's not worth it. Focus your energy on placing a different piece.

Protecting Traverses

Though rarely at risk of taking a dangerous fall, the second is in potential jeopardy following a traverse. When leading a traverse, establish placements adequate to protect your follower from a long *pendulum* fall, should he or she lose footing *(Illustrations: 1 and 2 previous page)*. Consider that following a traverse isn't much different than leading it. So place protection frequently, especially if the second's skill level is less than yours.

My partner once led a fairly easy pitch that involved a long but non-technical traverse. Guessing it'd be as easy for me as it was for him, he decided to forgo placing much protection to save time—black clouds were forming, threatening rain. When it came my turn to climb, it poured buckets. With slippery rock underfoot, it took all the chutzpah I possessed to cross that unprotected traverse without having a complete meltdown. It remains one of my most frightening climbing memories.

ROPE MANAGEMENT

Rope Positioning & Clipping

If you've led sport climbs, you have probably mastered these techniques. If you haven't, bolted sport routes provide the ideal setting to practice them.

If properly clipped, your lead rope passes through the carabiner on your piece toward you from the direction of the wall, *(Illustration: 1, top left)* leading directly to your tie-in knot. If you are about to traverse to the right, place the gate of the carabiner facing left *(Illustration: 2, middle left)* (vice versa if you traverse left *(Illustration: 3, bot-*

Rope Positioning

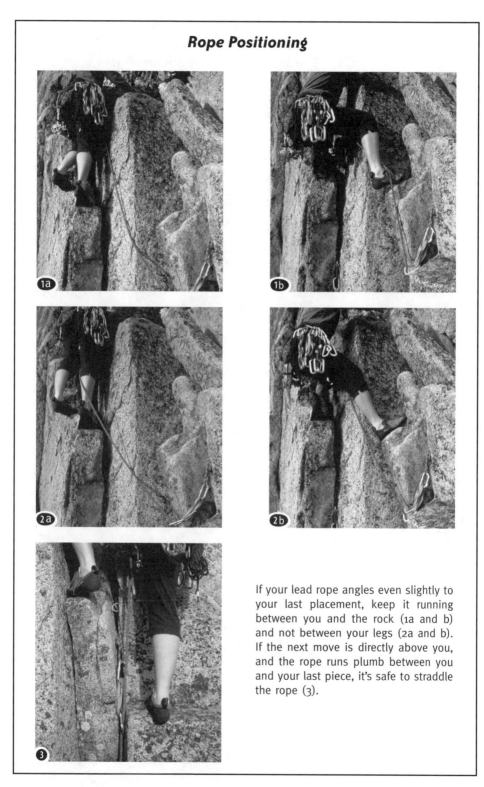

If your lead rope angles even slightly to your last placement, keep it running between you and the rock (1a and b) and not between your legs (2a and b). If the next move is directly above you, and the rope runs plumb between you and your last piece, it's safe to straddle the rope (3).

tom left). An improperly "back-clipped" rope could could unclip from the carabiner during a fall.

During my first several years of trad leading I fell upside down a few times. I didn't understand why, and my partners were baffled, too. I discovered later that the rope had been positioned behind my leg, and had

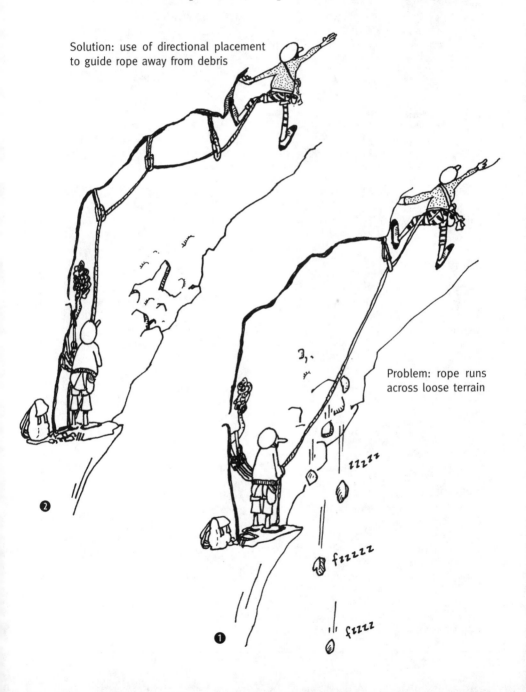

Solution: use of directional placement to guide rope away from debris

Problem: rope runs across loose terrain

flipped me upside down upon falling. Vigilant rope monitoring requires good judgment and helps prevent such mishaps. Pay attention to the rope's position as you continuously change yours relative to it. With the rope running straight down to your last piece, there's not much risk of getting it caught behind your leg and flipping you over; if the protection is directly below, it's safe to straddle the rope. If the rope angles even slightly to your last piece, keep the rope running between you and the rock; don't let it go between your legs and cross over the back of one of them. *(Photos: sidebar page 121).*

Directionals

Trad routes occasionally travel over sharp or loose terrain and follow crack systems with an appetite for rope. Whenever possible, scout for locations where you can place a directional piece to divert your lead line away from loose debris *(Illustrations: 1 and 2, left)*, sharp edges, and rope-masticating cracks. Deep roof cracks in particular are notorious for eating lead lines. Such a fate can usually be avoided by placing a piece at the lip.

MOVEMENT

Testing Holds

Trad rock can be loose and unstable. Before committing your entire weight to a suspect hold, test it first. Thump it with your palm, then ease onto it. This is good practice particularly at climbing areas that are new to you.

Rhythm & Flow

Beginner leaders have a tendency to *sew it up*—that is, place a lot of lead protection. While it's good considering the harsh learning curve, excessive gear placement can interfere with the natural flow of climbing movement. When I was still sewing it up after 10 years of leading, a valued mentor suggested I make a few more moves between pieces, generating necessary momentum to launch my body more smoothly from hold to hold. I soon discovered the value of this advice. Place gear thoughtfully and carefully, but try not to overprotect.

Climber: Mark Wilford

Years Trad Free Climbing: 28

Average Trad Lead Ability:
      5.11+/5.12-

Favorite Trad Climbing Area(s):
      Don't have one—I get
      most excited visiting an
      area I've never been
      before.

Most Respected Trad Free Climbers:
      John Bacher,
      Reinhold Messner

Photo by Barry Blanchard, Mark Wilford Collection

A Skill To Reduce Risk of Falling

When leading on trad climbs, make every attempt not to fall—make it your ethic and style. Learn when and how to rest on a pitch. Find stances where you can **shake out** and body positions that are conducive to resting (e.g. straight-arm hangs on crack sections). If you get out on a pitch and start getting tired, down-climb to the last stance and rest. If you do get to a point where you feel you're going to fall, still do your best to down-climb as far as you possibly can. Even if you can't reach the last good resting stance, you may be able to reduce the length of your fall. Don't grab the rope if you do fall—you'll only get burned. Down-climbing can be practiced on boulders close to the ground. This is an essential skill for trad leaders often overlooked by the novice in favor of techniques resulting directly in upward progress. Don't be fooled; if you fall and injure yourself, you're not going anywhere but down.

As a young climber I practiced down-climbing to get out of harm's way both on high boulder problems and on scary testpieces in Eldorado Canyon. Later I was able to apply these skills to alpine climbs. One instance that comes to mind is an experience on Mt. Alberta in the Canadian Rockies. This mountain forced me to down-climb hundreds of feet on my first failed attempt. Being able to safely retreat off a 4000' climb gave me the confidence to try again, and succeed on my second attempt.

—Mark Wilford

Energy Conservation

"Often resting is an art requiring ingenuity and experience, and on many difficult routes discovering ways to rest is as much a part of the problem as the actual climbing."

—*Royal Robbins*

Conserve energy by making the most of each rest opportunity. If a good stance isn't available, try to cop a rest with some creative body positioning. A straight-arm hang *(Photo: top right)* off a jam or handhold allows you to rest by shifting weight from your muscles to your skeletal system, and stemming *(Photo: middle right)* lets your legs share the weight burden with your lower body. On flaring cracks, try to relieve an overworked upper body by back-stepping (like you would in a chimney) *(Photo: bottom right)*. On overhanging terrain, try turning your hip perpendicular to the rock to better allow your feet to support your weight. The more climbing you do, the more intuitive your resting positions become.

Straight-arm hanging

Down-Climbing

The value of honed down-climbing skills isn't obvious until you're up there on the sharp end: you've botched a sequence of moves and are too gassed to plug in a piece. Remembering you're not on a sport route, you consider that "letting go" is not a favorable option—especially having just placed a marginal micro-cam, with a ledge looming close below. After a deep breath, begin carefully reversing your moves one by one. When you've safely reached the ledge, you can take a rest while rethinking the moves and getting a piece ready to fire in on your second try. Save "letting go" as a tactic for sport climbing. At that point of despair where you know you're facing a fall, try to reverse your moves to the last stable stance before giving up. Although we protect ourselves as best we can on lead, falling is always risky.

Stemming

Hanging

If you can't go on without a rest and decide to hang (take tension) on a piece, be certain that it's solid enough to hold body weight. If it's the only piece between you and the ground or a ledge, quickly plug in another for backup. Not a good habit to get into, some trad climbers

Back-stepping

even consider hanging "bad style." But sometimes it may be a safer choice than falling. Don't head up on lead with the mind-set that you can always hang on a piece when you tire; that option won't always exist. When protection is sparse or the climb is runout, a cavalier attitude won't serve you. Depend, instead, on your good downclimbing skills.

Backing Off

To retreat from, or *back off*, a single-pitch route, you can have your belayer lower you, only if the route is fairly direct, you haven't used more than half your rope, and you're at a solid piece of protection from which to be lowered. Unless your partner wants to finish the pitch, keep in mind that you must leave this piece, cleaning the others as you descend. Leaving a second piece is wise, so you're not trusting your life to just one. If you are more than halfway up the pitch, or the route traverses such that being lowered isn't an option, retreat becomes more complex. With adequate protection options, you might consider aiding your way to the top, or at least through the crux. To accomplish this, however, you may need more hardware and slings than you have. If you think you can make it, girth hitch several slings together to use as makeshift étriers and off you go. To best cope with this type of situation, become familiar with basic aid-climbing techniques *before* pushing your limits on trad free climbs. And on a difficult route, always consider how committed you are to the summit once you've used half the rope.

When retreat is necessary, climbers using double ropes (see Chapter 8) have less to worry about than those leading on a single line. No matter the length of the pitch, you can usually retreat with relative ease (unless the route traverses significantly) because you can tie two ropes together to rappel.

FALLING

Several schools exist regarding falling on trad lead. When I learned in the early '80s in Yosemite, the motto was simply DON'T FALL. With equipment technology not as advanced as today and many routes involving runouts, risks were greater then. Besides the technological handicap, in a regional sense falling happened to be considered bad style. There was pressure in the Valley to keep both your capabilities and limitations in check. Many trad free climbers still climb by the "no fall" adage (and may stay alive longer because of it).

The newer school of IF YOU'RE NOT FALLING YOU'RE NOT PROGRESSING was probably born out of the sport-climbing revolution that pushed free climbing standards. Climbers today who get their start in the gym or at sport crags learn that falling involves few risks and is an integral component of progressing. When these climbers cross over to trad climbing, this ideal, however tempered, remains a formative one in their conciousnesses.

My current philosophy lies somewhere between the two, with a tendency toward the "don't fall" school that probably reflects my climbing roots. Yet it also stems from a personal experience of a trad lead fall years ago where I overreached my capabilities. My piece was good, as was my belayer, and I only fell a few feet. Still, my tailbone was dislocated skittering across a small bulge and today I live with arthritis in my coccyx. I am cautious about pushing my limits now and recognize that a leader fall of *any* length can be dangerous.

Hazards

Falls happen regardless of your philosophy. As a new leader, it is your responsibility to understand the risks, learn to identify potential hazards, and do what you can to minimize them.

Place protection in key locations to avoid striking obstacles, even when climbing is easy. Never underestimate your potential to slip, break a hold, or lose your balance at any time on any climb. Look out for potential falls onto low-angle slabs and into dihedrals, and use caution when climbing directly above ledges and the ground.

As previously described, erroneous rope positioning increases your risk of being flipped upside-down during a lead fall. Maintain awareness of proper rope positioning to prevent such falls, and wear a helmet to reduce the risk of serious head injury should one occur.

Highest fall factor—there are no placements between belayer and leader

If you know you're about to peel, quickly ascertain the rope isn't wrapped around your leg and that your last piece (if you can see it) is stable and appropriately clipped. Warn your belayer, face the wall, and, catlike, cushion your fall with flexed legs. In some situations it may be advantageous to push yourself out and away from the rock, hopefully reducing the risk of catching an appendage on an obstacle during your flight.

Most instances of equipment failure on lead are due to user error. An improperly placed or poorly runnered piece of protection rips out, a rope running across a razor-sharp edge severs, the rope unclips from a quickdraw carabiner—all are preventable scenarios. Make the most of your equipment by understanding its limitations, cultivating keen protection placement skills, and paying attention on lead. In addition, study fall force potentials explained in the following paragraphs and place pieces with the most holding power in high force scenarios.

The Physics of Falling

Your equipment is subject to differing degrees of force depending on the circumstances of each fall. Many variables exist, including the fall distance, the rope length in use, the lead climber's weight, and the amount of time during which energy generates and dissipates. Use this information to make safe choices on lead to help minimize forces whenever possible. Continue reading for a simplified discussion of how some of these forces are gauged.

Fall Factor

Because analyzing loads and forces in relation to falling is a complex process with many variables, a method was devised to calculate the relative severity of falls instead. This method determines fall factors, taking into account the fall distance and the length of the rope that absorbs its force. To calculate it, divide the length of a fall by the amount of rope out. The highest forces are generated on multipitch routes when a fall without protection between belayer and leader occurs; this worst-case scenario results in the maximum fall factor of 2 *(Illustration: opposite page)*. By placing gear as early as possible after leaving a multipitch belay, this can be avoided (see Chapter 6). The more protection and rope out, the lower the potential fall factor. Ideally, you want to keep potential fall factors at 0.5 *(Illustration: right)*. Although terrain and gear availability might dictate otherwise, make this your goal. Review the formula on page 116 and do what you can to minimize fall factor potentials based on this ideal.

Impact Force

A lead climber's weight and acceleration in any given fall determine actual force exerted, and are together termed the *impact force*. In theory, and in research and development tests in which the average laboratory lead climber weighs 176 lbs, all falls of the same fall factor generate the same impact force. Impact forces in the real world, however, vary according to the climber's weight, the amount of friction in the system or between the climber and the rock (terrain angle), the age of the rope, and the rope elongation rating. In addition, impact force is buffered by knots being tightened and unanchored belayers lifted. Though impact force can affect other aspects of the roped climbing system, most importantly it affects your rope and protection.

Your rope's ability to stretch and absorb energy allows it to greatly reduce impact forces. Prior to the invention of the dynamic rope, pioneers of the sport climbed on static lines without this important feature.

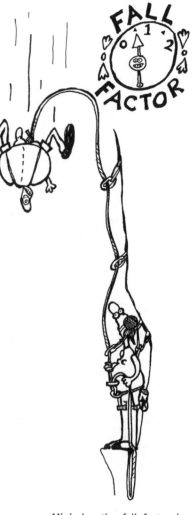

Minimize the fall factor by placing protection early and often.

Modern climbing rope specifications allow a maximum impact force of 12kN (2700 lbs) with a fall factor of 1.78. A seven-fall rating indicates the rope can withstand seven UIAA-rated falls[9] at this fall factor before breaking. All ropes are tested to breaking, so we know that they do. If your rope undergoes one severe fall (with a fall factor approaching 2) or a few falls with fall factors above 1, it may be time to retire it. After any significant fall, let your rope recover 5-10 minutes from its stretching and heating. If it can be done safely, untie from the rope and retie into it, to restore your knot's ability to absorb energy. (See Chapter 3, for more information on rope care and retirement.)

In relation to protection, impact force matters most when your pro is marginal and a reduction in potential fall force could prevent your piece from failing. Although you have little control over impact force, you can attach a load-limiter to a dicey piece, request a *dynamic belay* (where the belayer deliberately allows slippage of some rope through the belay device), or lead on a newer rope. As discussed previously, forgoing a base belay also reduces potential impact force by allowing the movement of the belayer to absorb some of the energy generated during a fall. Each of these options does, however, result in slightly longer falls. If you are facing a potentially injurious fall, use caution. Although utilizing one of these tactics may prove a worthy trade-off, perform a careful situational analysis first. (Some lead climbers carry load-limiters exclusively for clipping manky bolts they might be forced to use. This is a great idea considering how many ancient bolts are out there.)

Impact Impulse

The length of time during which energy is generated and dissipated on systems, rope, belayer, and climber is known as the *impact impulse*. The longer the fall, the greater it is. Though the impact force of a 10' fall with 10' of rope out (Fall Factor=1) generates the same peak impact force as a 100' fall with 100' of rope out, the impact forces last much longer with the 100' *whipper*, placing greater demands on climber, belayer, and protection. By placing gear frequently—even on easy ground—you can reduce the impulse impact in the event of a fall.

Practice Falls

If you're feeling gutsy and want to experience a lead fall on top-rope, locate a steep rock expanse on the upper section of a long pitch. This stretch should be free of ledges, *dihedrals*, slabs, or other obstacles. You'll need a second belayer to catch your fall on the lead line; your top-rope belayer provides slack when you're ready to fall and acts as backup. Once you have confirmed with the lead-line belayer that you are indeed on belay, climb half a body length above your piece and prepare to fall. Ask your top-rope belayer to feed out just enough slack to let the lead line catch your fall when you're ready to launch. Then go for it. If you're successful, your piece will hold and you'll land right-side up, having experienced a short leader fall. If your piece fails you'll fly slightly farther, until the top-rope belayer catches your fall on the top-rope. Although risks are significantly reduced, a practice fall is *still* dangerous. Be absolutely certain the fall occurs high above the ground on steep terrain free of any hazardous rock features or obstacles, and wear your helmet.

ESTABLISHING THE BELAY ANCHOR

Location

On traditional routes it's not always obvious at the top of the pitch where to set up your belay anchor. Sometimes the location is indicated on the topo, or on-site by the presence of pre-drilled bolts, slings, and/or other types of fixed protection. If it isn't obvious, find out from your belayer how much rope is remaining so you don't climb too high. There's nothing worse than assuming the belay ledge is just 10 feet up and then feeling an annoying tug on your waist and hearing your partner yell, "That's it! There's no more rope!" On long pitches, before leaving the ground, I request my partner let me know when I'm down to 25' (8-9m). If you're low on rope and have no idea where the designated belay is, look for a location offering the best possible protection. While a fairly big stance makes everyone more comfortable, what really matter is your ability to set up a SERENE anchor

(Chapter 4) with the pieces remaining on your rack. If you can't, carefully down-climb to a location where you can. In this case you may have to do another short pitch to reach the actual summit, but it will be worth it to have a solid anchor.

Fixed Belay Anchors

Although it's tempting to hastily clip into a fixed anchor (see Chapter 4) after completing a demanding lead, first examine it carefully and make sure it's as close to SERENE as possible. Set up your own anchor if you don't like what you see. If the fixed anchor doubles as a rappel station, avoid clipping into the chains or the nest of nylon webbing linking the bolts together. Rather, clip your carabiners directly into each bolt. If necessary, cut away old slings to make room for your 'biners; keep the blade far away from your climbing rope—especially if the rope is tensioned.

As you break into traditional leading, the basic principles and guidelines presented in this chapter will help you safely master the difficult learning curve. It's a lot of information? Yes, but remember that, besides the protocol, it's your cumulative experience from a lot of time on the rock that's going to save your butt out there.

"Good decisions are the result of experience; experience is the result of bad decisions." I don't know who first coined this adage, but it emphasizes aptly the importance of hands-on experience for new trad leaders. With more overall experience you'll realize the challenge is lifelong. With a few years of consistent practice—as your mind-body learns this unique language—trad leading can become second nature. But leave the crags for a season, and you'll experience a rapid decline in both mental and physical fluency revived only after you return to basics.

As your comfort level increases on single-pitch trad leads, you'll probably experience a yearning toward multipitch lead climbing. Chapter 6 discusses how to build on your single-pitch leading skills so that you can cope effectively with the challenges of long routes.

Chapter 6

The Multipitch Adventure

Reaching from a distant horizon, welcome beams of sunlight soften the bite of dawn's chill and beckon your muscles into action. Through misting breath you peer up toward the steeple of white granite towering above. Your partner's groggy "On belay" initiates your ascent like a contractual agreement. Stepping onto the wall you make the first of thousands of moves that, with the grace of the mountain, will offer a moment of summit glory later in the day.

Several pitches up, high off the ground, the real adventure in trad free climbing begins. With your necessary lasting endurance and commitment, steep exposures, *hanging belays*, weather, and altitude create the thrill of multipitch exploit. This chapter explores leading and belaying on long trad routes, as well as the tasks of preparation, the approach, objective hazards, anchors, organization, and the descent.

Bill McChesney

PREPARATION

Before embarking on a long free route as a full-fledged leading partner, some groundwork is necessary. Many of the tasks are similar to basic prep for the single-pitch trad climb: route choice, partners, and gear. But because of the complexity of multipitch routes, these issues require more forethought and energy.

Route Choice

Since retreat is complex on long climbs, the routes you choose must honestly reflect your team's collective, lead-ability level—not just in terms of ratings but also of terrain. For instance, off-width cracks are notorious enigmas for new leaders, even if moderately rated (see Chapter 8). A 5"-wide (12.5cm) crack rated at 5.8 could be significantly more difficult than a hand crack of the same rating, if your prior experience on wide terrain has been minimal. And it may be difficult to protect unless you have a glut of large gear (which most new leaders do not). Runouts also challenge new leaders. It often takes years to develop the mental capability to effectively cope with them. Many long routes involve off-width or chimney sections and even the most popular ones have short terrain sections difficult to protect. Before you commit to such a route, be absolutely certain one member of your team is up to the challenge.

Also evaluate if the number of available daylight hours is adequate to complete the length of the proposed route. Schedule extremely long routes—particularly those involving long approaches or descents and higher difficulty levels—within a month or two of the summer solstice, and a few days prior to the night of a full moon if the possibility exists you may be walking out in the dark.

Although some long routes are located in popular climbing areas, where a shout for help might be easily heard by tourists or other climbers who can notify rescue personnel should medical and/or retreat assistance be required, many

Dave Nettle Collection

Typical Sierra Nevada backcountry approach

are not. These secluded *backcountry* settings, miles or even days from civilization, require that your team prepare for self-sufficiency and understand the ramifications of a mishap. Be able to provide detailed answers to these questions:

• Am I prepared to take full responsibility for myself and my partner?

• Do I have a sound understanding of self-rescue techniques?

• Do I have the proper equipment and apparel?

• Am I trained in first aid?

• How will I initiate an evacuation if necessary?

Because loose rock is also commonly encountered by backcountry climbers, wear a helmet and move cautiously to prevent dislodging it. After only climbing popular easily-accessed routes, you'll find the backcountry is another world in terms of quality standards. Yet, what you give up in rock stability is a fair trade for the solitude and natural beauty you experience in wilderness climbing.

With a proposed route high in the mountains, consider the environmental implications and adjust your goals accordingly. An increase in altitude affects your endurance and strength because your body labors to compensate for lower concentrations of oxygen. Most people tire more easily at high altitudes. Since I regularly climb at 7400' (2312m), when I read a topo indicating a 5.8 pitch above 12000' (3750m) I know it's going to feel more like 5.9. If you're a lowlander climbing at sea level, the difference will feel much greater. Altitude illnesses, which generally don't occur under 8000' (2500m), are discussed later in this chapter.

Partner Choice

Be selective when choosing partners for multipitch climbs. Partnerships must be cohesive—particularly where limited daylight or changeable weather requires a breakneck pace without sacrificing safety. In these situations mastery in rope- and gear-handling skills is crucial, so look for someone experienced. If your partner isn't, choose a shorter and easier route. Choose a partner with whom you have done single pitches, have a good rapport, and whose abilities you know well and trust completely.

Don't be afraid of backing out of a multipitch climb at the last minute, if your intuition strongly prompts you. I once drove four hours toward the trailhead of a Sierra backcountry route with a potential partner, but turned the car around because a voice told me this person wasn't going to cut it. Our conversations had led me to conclude that I couldn't trust this fellow with my life. He was angry and I felt guilty, but I made the right choice.

Weather

Studying weather patterns prior to embarking upon a long route will save you time and frustration should the outlook be grim. As a new leader, if the forecast is iffy your best bet is to reschedule. If I'm planning on climbing in an unfamiliar area, I'll check the Internet for a local weather forecast. I may even follow up with a call to a climbing shop in the nearest community. Exercise caution when reports indicate a drop in barometric pressure. Learn to read the wind and sky to recognize when bad weather is approaching, so that a descent can be initiated before precipitation occurs. In the northern hemisphere, a shift in wind direction to the east or southeast may indicate an approaching low-pressure system. High-altitude cirrus clouds, which are typically identified by feathery narrow bands or thin wispy patches, are also common indicators of potential precipitation *(Photo: left)*. Be wary of cirrus clouds that form a tight halo around the moon or sun, and/or begin to lower and thicken.

Understanding thunderstorm cycles is also helpful—particularly in mountain

High-altitude cirrus clouds indicate potential precipitation.

and desert environments. Such cycles can last several days, and are generally accompanied by a high-pressure system in surrounding areas. Although thunderstorms can occur without warning, they're generally preceded by a gradual buildup of cumulus clouds *(Photo: right)* a few days before. These clouds, billowy and bold, usually appear in the after-noon, but they occur earlier and earlier each day until a full-blown storm cuts loose.

Cumulus clouds

In any mountain environment be prepared for thunderstorms by always packing lightweight rain gear. For extra insurance, bring another rope (or climb with double ropes) in case retreat becomes inevitable. Some climbers carry an 8mm rope religiously on long routes, used only for emergency descents. Because a rope this small tends to be squirrely and unmanageable at its full length, carry it in a pack. Another weather-beating tip is to get an early *alpine start*, giving you several hours to climb before most thunderstorms develop. One partner of mine insists on being off mountain routes by noon, no matter what the forecast. This is a smart philosophy, particularly for beginners.

Hot temperatures are as likely as rain or snow to put a glitch in your progress on long routes, particularly in temperatures above 90°F (32.2°C). With high humidity the problem is worse. Not uncommon for long-route climbers in warmer climes, heat exhaustion quickly turns a capable partner into a tired, dizzy, vomiting mess. Although this condition is not particularly dangerous, untreated it can lead to deadly heat stroke. If your chosen route is in an area experiencing a hot spell, consider rescheduling your climb. If you decide to climb, don't forget sunscreen—particularly on highly reflective white rock like limestone and granite—and copious amounts of water.

The Pack

Although carrying a pack can be either helpful or a hindrance, the more water and clothing you need, the more you'll appreciate it. On routes less than 5 or 6 pitches I often forgo a pack. I hang water bottle and shoes on my harness loops, and tie a lightweight rain jacket around my waist. Some outerwear manufacturers make lightweight jackets from waterproof but breathable fabrics that fold into themselves for nice little packages you can clip to a harness loop. And if I can manage it, I also bring my light all-terrain sandals soled with sticky rubber for short, non-technical descents.

For climbs that take a full day, a pack is almost always a necessity. Choose one with minimal waist padding so it can ride above your waist belt and stay out of the way of your gear loops and chalk bag. Consider, though, that a pack without waist padding can be uncomfortable on a long approach, when water bottles are full and the trail is generally uphill. A pack capacity of 1500-2000 cubic inches is adequate for most daylong routes. Avoid a frame pack, although a minimal internal stay might be okay. Choose one made of an abrasion-resistant fabric—particularly on the bottom—with sturdy stitching. Forget external mesh pouches, ski loops, and ice ax and crampon holders (although loops for a single tool are handy for approaches and descents in alpine settings). Since you may have to hand-haul the pack when negotiating a chimney, the fewer external features the less likely it will get stuck. Some packs with gear loops on waist belts, which are mainly designed for ski mountaineering or moderate alpine climbing, can sometimes work well on long free-rock routes but might pose problems should hauling be necessary. Non-zippered top-loading packs are my personal choice; I particularly like them because if necessary I can sandwich in more gear between the top flap and the main compartment. Other climbers prefer zippered-loading packs because without buckles they are less likely to snag if hauled. Be sure your pack has a sturdy haul loop for clipping off at belays and hauling.

Food & Water

Dehydration produces alarming dysfunction in an otherwise capable climber. Scientific studies indicate that as little as 5 percent dehydration can cause up to 30 percent reduction in athletic performance. Although you're rarely able to achieve optimal hydration on long routes, strive to meet healthy standards. Before a long route, drink a large volume of water. After your initial drink, the International Sportsmedicine Institute recommends ½-⅔ ounce of water per pound of body weight per day (around 3-4 quarts daily for the average-sized person). Though my rations rarely match these ideals—even when climbing in the front-country—I do my best. On hot, humid days I carry more. For routes with long descents, I carry iodine tablets to treat lake or stream water so I won't have to conserve it for the trek down.

I also carry on my harness a small half-liter water bottle (I refill from larger bottles), rigged with a keeper loop from webbing secured with duct tape. I'm usually most parched after finishing a lead, and it's nice to not have to wait for the second, cleaning the pitch and reaching the belay, to retrieve water from inside the pack. Be considerate of your partner by not guzzling more than your share; it's hard to forgive, particularly on scorching days.

Adding sports drink mixes to some of your water aids in electrolyte replacement on long climbs. Electrolytes help metabolize carbos and boost muscle function, reducing muscle cramps and enhancing muscle cell contraction. Most importantly, they relieve dehydration through sodium replacement. Sodium is lost during exercise via sweating. For the most beneficial absorption rate, create these cocktails with no more than 8 percent drink mix. If you have a sensitive stomach, avoid straight glucose and sucrose mixes like Gatorade, and look for a brand such as Cytomax and Gluconaid in which the glucose comes from glucose polymers (maltodextrins).

Calories provide necessary energy for maximum performance. Starting off by eating a good breakfast is absolutely key for lasting endurance. Likewise, a hearty meal after your climb will aid in recovery. On the route, bring snacks that are high in complex carbohydrates with moderate amounts of fat and protein. Avoid foods extremely high in protein or fat that compromise performance by rerouting blood from the muscles to the digestive tract. This is why you may feel sluggish after gobbling a handful of nuts and a few slices of cheese and salami at the belay. Sugar alone is great for a quick burst of energy but won't sustain you for long, and neither will simple carbohydrates. Whole-wheat bagels, hummus, and whole-wheat fig bars are good choices.

As an alternative or supplement, bring along several energy gel packets and a few complex carbohydrate energy bars to consume en route. I prefer Clif Shots and Clif Bars. Clif Shots have added electrolytes and are easy to consume even if you're not feeling hungry. Some have a small amount of caffeine as well, proven by researchers to boost athletic performance. Clif Bars are a tasty form of complex carbos that neither harden nor melt with varying temperatures. Wash these down with a few ounces of water to encourage digestion.

No matter what food choices you make, don't starve yourself on any long route or you'll reap fatigue as your reward. Says Marc Twight in *Extreme Alpinism*, "...descending into calorie debt is counterproductive, no matter what the justification. Failing to maintain calorie intake may translate in the backcountry into hitting the wall.... Make sure your partner eats, too, because there's nothing worse than having one guy strong, and the other weak."[10]

Gear

Partners should review and be in agreement on equipment beforehand. On multipitch routes only one rack is necessary. Take either partner's rack, or a selection of pieces chosen from both partners'. If your partner has a rack of Hexes and you're most familiar with SLCDs, you'll be sorry when you discover this after hiking a distance to the base.

What if your partner is a more experienced leader, is extremely familiar with the route, and feels comfortable with a rack composed of half the gear you usually bring on lead? A friend of mine had this very experience not long ago when a strong, longtime Yosemite Valley local invited him to climb the renowned Astroman with him one morning. After they hiked to the base, the local, who has lapped this Valley testpiece many times, pulls out the "rack"—a few nuts and a half-dozen cams. He sets off on the familiar route, climbing swiftly and confidently, placing only a few pieces. When my friend attempts the notoriously long and difficult "Endurance Corner" with the scrawny rack, his confidence is shaken. Even though he climbed the route once before, he realizes this gear isn't sufficient for him to lead with comfort. When the two reluctantly retreat, my friend curses himself for not checking out his partner's gear, and the local feels awful. Not trying to *sandbag* my friend, he just had a skewed perception—because of his skill level and route familiarity—of what an adequate rack would be.

Information you glean from the topo, guidebook, and other resources help you determine what gear you'll need for lead protection. If the topo is vague, come prepared with two of each standard-sized piece up to 4-5" (10-12.5cm), and a few extras to outfit belays (unless they're bolted). If your resources indicate a long section requiring one particular size, you might need to borrow gear from friends (common on desert routes where long, uniform, parallel cracks are the norm). If a wide section high up on the route requires large pieces of protection, don't skimp because of their bulk; carry them in the pack until you need them.

Long trad routes, often linking several "weaknesses" on a rock face, tend to wander. For this reason, come prepared with several 22-24" (55-60cm) runners. The number you carry will vary depending on the route's composition, as well as on individual pitch lengths. When you're learning it's better to bring too many, since webbing weighs so little. I carry from six to eight runners on the average multipitch route, and a few more if most pitches are rope stretchers—150' (50m) and up. If the route appears fairly direct, I carry them as quickdraws (see Chapter 3). If the route meanders significantly, I carry at least half open their full length over my shoulder opposite the rack. You should also bring along at least one 44" (110cm) sling to protect traverses, runner natural protection, or tie in faraway anchor components to your other pieces. Two of these are optimal on wandering routes but, on blocky mountain routes, bring three or four.

Because many carabiners are required for belay anchors in the multipitch scenario, they aren't available for use on lead. So, rack accordingly by bringing along more than you would for a single-pitch climb.

You need a second rope (or "trail line") on a multipitch route, if the descent involves rappels longer than half the length of your lead rope. Yet, regardless of the descent, bringing an extra rope on long climbs provides backup insurance if you run into trouble. If your primary lead rope is damaged, your trail line can be used for leading, provided it is of sufficient diameter (see Chapter 3). If you retreat by rappelling the line of ascent with two ropes, it will take half the time and require less gear loss for anchors. Two ropes or one—it's a personal decision that should be dictated by your experience and relative commitment to the route. Many teams forgo a second rope (unless necessary for the standard descent) in deference to speed and experience. But if you're new to the game, bring a second rope on all multipitch routes to increase your odds for a safe adventure.

Consider carrying unruly, small-diameter ropes under 8mm uncoiled inside the bottom of the pack until needed. Although this increases the follower's burden, rope-management problems are kept to a minimum.

If you find yourself drawn to long, moderate back-country routes, consider building a specialized rack with lightweight gear: asymmetrical featherweight carabiners, Friends (instead of Camalots) or, even lighter, Hexes and Tri-Cams (instead of SLCDs). Be sure your partner is agreeable to such equipment, and that both of you know how to use it properly. (Many climbers today are unfamiliar with placing Hexes and Tri-Cams.) Particularly at higher altitudes, you'll be grateful for the weight savings.

Cooperative Racking System

Before getting started, work out an agreeable racking scheme with your partner. If you are alternating (swinging) leads, an ideal arrangement is for both climbers to carry separate gear slings. As the second cleans each pitch, he or she can re-rack equipment to his or her own specifications, in preparation for taking on the next lead. When you both reach the belay anchor, there's minimal gear swapping (unless the pitch was short or little protection placed). If racking arrangements differ between partners, little time is lost reorganizing gear.

If you're the sole leader, this system requires switching gear slings at the belay. In this case, make sure the follower is familiar with your racking preferences and can tolerate the same-sized gear sling, if it's not easily adjusted.

Another option is to share one gear sling between two partners. If you choose this method, adapt to subtle differences in your partner's racking habits and strive for a uniform approach to carrying gear. If you're flexible, sharing a gear sling will pose fewer problems and require less time at the belay. A final note to those who prefer racking only on harness loops: you're going to spend a lot of time swapping and rearranging gear at belays.

The Approach

Getting to the base of your route could be as simple as stumbling out of your tent or car and walking five minutes on a flat, manicured trail. In other cases, the approach might require miles of cross-country travel across talus and scree terrain, over snowfields, or up technically ambiguous Class 3 and 4 ledge systems. Miles of seemingly flat, off-trail hiking in desert settings might require keen navigational skills to avoid steep gullies and ravines, which are often hidden by the one-dimensional mirage that desert presents from distant views. For long approaches that don't follow maintained hiking trails, obtain a good area topo map, and bring a compass in case you lose your way.

For adequate time to complete the route and descend as soon as possible, hit the trail early. Though I hate getting up early, words of a longtime mentor caution me against snoozing through the pre-dawn hours: "You should find yourself on the approach in the dark, not the descent." Always bring extra batteries and a bulb for your headlamp and, when you've finished using it, temporarily disconnect the battery so it won't turn on inside the pack.

If the approach takes hours longer than you planned, you may reach the base wondering whether to continue with your ascent, or retreat and do the route another day.

Use your best judgment: realistically assess the weather and the daylight hours; think about the "what ifs," allowing time to get off-route or briefly lost on the descent. Try to sort out the tangled strands of ambition that tell you the summit must be attained at any cost.

MOVING UP

Route Finding

Finding your way on long trad climbs is a bit like a detective piecing together many clues to solve a great mystery. Depending on their traffic and terrain, some routes may pose greater puzzles. Climbs on remote or obscure crags present navigational challenges that popular routes with mellow approaches do not. Unfortunately, misinformation is so common that a team must ultimately rely on good navigational skills and intuition to assemble the puzzle.

Longtime Colorado trad-specialist Mark Wilford recommends studying a long route first from a distance to get a basic perspective of where the climb goes. Once on the climb he points out, you won't have a good perspective of the climbing above you: "After viewing the route, memorize features such as dihedrals, ledge systems, and overhangs so you will know what to look for as you work your way up the climb."

If all evidence of human traffic disappears or the rock takes on a loose and lichen-covered texture, you may be off-route. Sometimes climbers are lured astray by a fixed piece or a sling that turns out to be a retreat anchor from a previous off-route party. Before you're too committed to an unintentional off-piste venture, be sure you don't make any moves that cannot be reversed. Use your down-climbing skills to return to the route or, if you have anchor options and enough rope, lower back to the belay. If you don't have enough rope, set up an anchor, bring your partner up, and put your heads together to determine the safest way for getting back on track.

Trail Line Management

Trailing a second rope is generally but not always entrusted to the follower. There are benefits and liabilities to each course of action. If the follower trails the second line, the leader is free from the burden of the extra weight. However, if the rope becomes stubbornly wedged in a crack or hooked on a flake, the follower must down-climb or be lowered to retrieve the stuck line and re-climb the pitch. If the leader trails the second rope and it gets stuck below, he or she can simply clip it off onto a piece for the follower to retrieve. In this scenario, the rope should be tied in at the lower belay as a backup until the follower begins climbing.

Whenever transferring a second line at the belay between partners, use extreme caution and recognize the cost of accidentally dropping it. Before unclipping it from your haul loop, first clip it off to the belay anchor. If you lose your second rope and the descent requires long rappels, you're in deep doo-doo.

THE BELAY

Anchors

Upon placing the first piece of an anchor system at the end of any pitch, immediately clip your lead line in temporarily. This helps prevent a longer fall should you lose your balance before tying into the completed anchor. Since you're still leading, don't tie off to, and weight, this one piece while finishing the rest of the anchor. To do so would be almost like trusting your life to one piece, particularly if your last one is far below. Simply clip it for pro, and remain "on lead" until the anchor is completed and ready.

Aside from the first and last anchors on a multipitch route, your belay anchors must be multidirectional (see Chapter 4). Although time consuming, you can wait for the second to arrive to place the anchor component that will withstand an upward or oblique force. (Upward forces are not an issue until a climber takes off leading the following pitch.) If you do, use a sling to clip it taut to either your harness or the masterpoint to avoid having to re-string your cordelette.

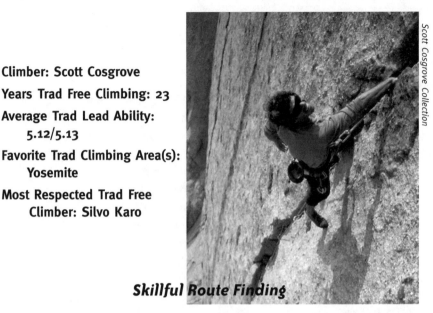

Scott Cosgrove Collection

Climber: Scott Cosgrove

Years Trad Free Climbing: 23

Average Trad Lead Ability:
   5.12/5.13

Favorite Trad Climbing Area(s):
   Yosemite

Most Respected Trad Free
   Climber: Silvo Karo

Skillful Route Finding

Route finding is an art, especially on multipitch routes. Approach the task as if you were the first ascent team. They didn't have a topo. They had to look for the most natural line up the rock.

Think simply. Watch a dog run up a rocky hillside. It will intuitively find the most obvious natural weakness and follow that path. As a trad leader, you'll do just that. Look for the largest series of holds in sight, and the path most worn. Watch out for "sucker" holds (a series of holds that lead nowhere) known as traps. These are easy to identify on more popular climbs. Often you'll see slings at the ends of traps where others lured there have eventually bailed.

Scope out the climb from the ground before navigating long routes. The pros use telescopes and binoculars to closely scan their climbing routes, but a keen trained eye will suffice for most. Look closely at routes you've already climbed and learn to identify the correct line of ascent from below. First learn to identify the largest, most obvious features—huge dihedrals, roofs, ledges, and foliage—and work from there to locate smaller features. Eventually you'll develop the ability to read the rock, identifying distant lines with relative ease. Like getting used to contour lines on regular topo maps, with practice, you can distinguish hills and valleys at a single glance.

Remain close to reachable, solid protection to stay alive on nebulous terrain. Don't commit to a line of holds unless you're sure it

Continued on next page

goes. Also, keep the pitch rating in mind and notice how it compares to that of lower climbing. Determine if the climbing is much too hard or easy for the grade. If so, stop and find the correct line. In addition to the largest holds, look for chalk and clean rock: on some types of rock, a subtle white streak is often present where traffic has worn lichen off popular routes; elsewhere you may notice black rubber streaks from climbing shoes.

Topos are only maps—don't be too dependent on them. Again, learn to spot your line from a distance. While on a route, always look ahead to identify the upper pitches. When in doubt, try to stay in control and coolheaded. Blindly surging forward off-route has resulted in many accidents. Always be ready to bail if you can't find a safe passage.

—Scott Cosgrove

Organization

Establishing an organized **belay station** is key to moving fast, and requires forethought. Before setting up the belay consider these factors:

• Where will you position yourself? What stance will provide the most comfortable belaying—the easiest stacking of the slack line as your partner ascends? How much of a leash will you need to be comfortable?

• Assess whether the rope to the second could run across loose pebbles or rocks presenting a potential hazard. If it could, give yourself a longer leash (more slack) so you'll be able, closer to the vertical relief, to keep the rope away from the debris.

• Will the masterpoint of your proposed anchor be at a sufficient height for use as a directional when belaying? (See "Belaying the Second" below.) A masterpoint nose-high or above is ideal.

• Where will you pile/flake the slack rope as your partner ascends? Where will the follower clip into the anchor? If your belay brake is on the right, plan for the slack line from belaying also on the right. Left-handers should pile their slack line on the left. If piling slack rope on one side is your only option, switch your brake hand to that side.

Avoid annoying entanglements at multipitch belays by proper equipment layering.

• Where will you place or hang the pack?

• If the second is trailing a rope, where will this line be stacked?

• Where will your partner sit, hang, or stand? Is this location good for easily exchanging gear? If you're swapping leads, can the next leader climb from the belay stance without becoming entangled in anchor components? *(Illustration: above)*

Consider each factor carefully and make appropriate decisions to ensure a smooth adventure. You develop good belay organization—particularly on hanging belays—with forethought plus a lot of experience.

Belaying the Second

When belaying the second, use the anchor as a directional to prevent your partner's weight from wrenching your body in a fall. Tie yourself in about an arm's length to the anchor, so that you're hanging or standing slightly below your masterpoint. Clipping into the cordelette *shelf* (Photo: top) prevents crowding at the masterpoint. Take a bight of the rope leading from your belay device (on your waist) to the follower, and clip it with a carabiner to the masterpoint. (Photo: middle) The drawback of this rig is a simple physics problem, known as an additive-pulley effect, in which loads on the directional are doubled when weighted. Another option is belaying with a Munter hitch and locking carabiner directly off the anchor (Photo: bottom). This method makes belay escape a cinch, and solves both the loading problem and the issue of additive-pulley effect. It does tend to twist the rope if you don't manage it properly, and cannot be used to belay a leader. If you have *any* question about

To anchor yourself to the cordelette shelf: above the knot creating the masterpoint, clip one of every two strands that is leading to each anchor component.

Re-directed waist belay

the integrity of your anchor, skip the directional and belay your partner off your body (harness). By making your body a part of the system, you provide an additional resource for energy absorption in a fall, relieving a sketchy anchor from the force. To do it comfortably, find a good stance wedged between two features for maximum stability; be certain the rope direction and your hand position is such that an unexpected weighting of the rope won't injury your hand or wrist.

As you belay the second up to the anchor, you have lots of slack line to manage. Rope management at the belay is crucial, not only for organizational purposes,

Munter belay off the masterpoint

On hanging belays, flake the slack rope, butterfly style on the taut rope.

Or flake it in a sling.

but to prevent the rope from getting stuck on features below. Keep the rope from dangling freely, unless the rock below is either overhanging or smooth (free of cracks or other features on which it could snag). If you're on a ledge, keep the rope in a neat pile beside you. At hanging belays, flake the rope butterfly-style on the taut rope between you and where you are tied into the anchor *(Photo: top left)*. Alternatively, you could flake it butterfly-style in a sling off a piece of your anchor system *(Photo: bottom left)*. If you're not swinging leads, always restack the rope before setting off on the next lead.

The Changeover

All about gear management and organization, the *changeover* takes place at the top of each pitch after the second reaches the stance. If your team is committed to moving efficiently and fast, an effective changeover can save precious time. Yet, for obvious reasons, it's at belays on long routes where climbers often succumb to mental and physical weariness. If you find yourself lagging during the changeover, snap out of your stupor; you'll have time to relax once your partner begins leading the next pitch (unless you're leading in blocks). According to the late climber Seth Shaw, "If you're not doing anything at the belay (changeover), you're being lame. Find a rope to flake, some gear to organize, or get your partner some water or food from the pack. Don't just stand there watching him do all the work." (Shaw was a talented climber from Utah, tragically killed on a serac in Alaska during the writing of this book.)

The following suggestions can make your changeovers smooth, efficient, and safe:

• John Hoffman, a retired Alpine Skills International (ASI) guide, says that when his partner reaches the belay he "goes verbal." An example might sound something like this: "Okay, I'm going to clip you in right here, and now you're off belay. All right, let me have the pack...here's the water—got it? I'm clipping the pack off over here—no, that'll be in the way of the lead line, but this works right here...okay, that's clipped off. Now, are you ready to give me some gear?" Verbalizing your actions reinforces your clarity and command of the system, and lets your partner know what's going on at the belay. When climbers tire and errors are most likely to occur, it also helps keep things straight, according to Hoffman.

• When the second arrives at the anchor, the belayer should direct him or her to a stance best suited to that climber's next task (belaying or leading). If the climber will remain the follower, tie him or her into the master-point and disengage your device. If this climber is going to lead the next pitch, tie your partner off to the master-point but leave your belay device engaged. If you are alternating leads and are on a fairly large stance (eliminating the climber's need to weight the rope), you can skip tying him or her into the anchor by keeping your belay device engaged, passing a bight through your locking carabiner, and tying a *mule knot* (see Chapter 7) for temporary security. While the climber remains on belay, with the device secured by the knot your hands are free for the changeover. When he or she is ready to climb, the mule knot is easily released for an immediate belay.

• Use the rope to clip into belay anchors whenever possible. Both climbers should carry a locking carabiner strictly for this purpose. Although some climbers tout the daisy chain for use in multiple-pitch anchoring situations, it's unnecessary gear when you can use the rope. Plus, on hanging belays, the dynamic stretch of rope when weighted is far more comfortable than webbing. The quick adjustability rope offers when used with the clove hitch is lost if you use a daisy chain (unless you use two locking carabiners, thus having to carry more gear). A daisy chain might be useful in these situations: when rope ends need to be swapped at the belay, either because one partner is doing all the leading or your party is leading in blocks (see below); or if you anticipate multiple rappels. Both scenarios require a method of remaining clipped to the anchors during transitions.

• Relieve the second of the pack, securing it temporarily into any component of the system, retrieve water and/or food as needed, and then secure it out of the way to one piece that accepts a downward force. Be sure it isn't lying against any part of the system that you need to access in the immediate future (such as the slack lead line). Never leave the pack unclipped from the anchor unless you're on a huge ledge.

• If you're swinging leads, the previous leader must transfer unused items quickly but carefully to the new one. If the former second has racked efficiently during cleaning, this step takes little time. When passing gear, hand your partner *one piece at a time* (Chapter 4). Don't let go unless you're certain he or she has a grip on the piece. Some climbers won't release their grip until they hear an affirmative "Got it."

• With the remaining rack available, now is the time to reinforce your anchor, if necessary. If your anchor is comprised of three pieces of the same size, consider that the lead rack is now void of that size—a potential handicap for the next leader. Swap pieces as necessary, and don't forget your upward pull component (see "Anchors," Chapter 4, and "The Belay," Chapter 6).

• If you led the prior pitch and will lead the next one, the rope must be restacked (so that the rope fed to you as you ascend is coming from the top of the pile rather than the bottom). You'll regret skipping this step, because untangling your partner's lead line single-handedly when he or she needs slack to move up or clip a piece is dangerous and unnerving. If one partner is leading every pitch on a long route, some teams prefer switching tie-in points (see "Leading in Blocks", below) to reflaking the rope at every changeover.

• Before leaving the belay anchor, the leader should clip into the equalized anchor point as his or her first piece (as long as the anchor is absolutely bomber). I've seen belayer injuries ranging from dislocated wrists to severe rope burns resulting from Factor 2 falls (see Chapter 5). In each case the leader failed to clip the belay anchor as his or her first piece, and the belayer was poorly positioned. If for any reason you do not clip the anchor as you begin your lead, make certain your belayer is positioned so that a Factor 2 fall won't injury him or her.

• Finally, check that the leader has all necessary gear, including the topo, and that the second has the nut tool (if you're sharing). If you're belaying, check the rear loops of your harness for gear you might have missed, and be sure the new leader has all the slings. If you're hauling a second rope, make sure you transfer it to the appropriate partner's haul loop.

Leading in Blocks

An alternative to swapping (or swinging) leads on multipitch routes involves leading in blocks. In this system each climber accepts leading responsibilities for several consecutive pitches. For example on a 10-pitch route, one climber agrees to lead pitches 1-5 and the other leads 6-10. Where swinging leads requires the follower jump directly into leading mode at each belay, this system gives each climber a chance to settle into his or her role. Though the pressure of continuous time on the sharp end can be exhaustive, some climbers prefer it to constant role changing. Just consider beforehand the burden of leading the final pitches after a tiring and possibly strenuous day.

To lead in blocks, climbers must either re-flake the rope after each pitch, or clip in at belays with a daisy chain (or a cow's tail) and a locker so that rope ends can be swapped at each belay. To eliminate constant tying and untying, secure the rope to your harness with two locking carabiners and a figure-eight on a bight (see Chapter 8). It makes trading ends a cinch.

OBJECTIVE HAZARDS

Objective hazards tend to increase on longer climbs. These factors are generally out of our control such as rain, snow, hail, lightning, rockfall, and high-altitude illness. You can, however, minimize their likelihood or impact through prevention, preparedness, and sound judgment.

Poor Weather

Encounters with rain, sleet, hail, or snow are not uncommon on long routes, particularly those in the mountain environments. Since they uncover a wild card that could instantly alter your progress on a long climb, climb prepared with appropriate clothing and an extra rope for a potential retreat.

In any area notorious for afternoon thundershowers, getting an early start helps ensure a safe and dry climbing experience. If there's a good trail to the base, use your headlamp and begin walking before sunrise; begin the route as the sun is rising. Your biggest concerns with rain or snow are exposure and potential hypothermia. If weather reports indicate a low-pressure system likely to bring precipitation, either choose a shorter climb with an easy *escape route* for a quick retreat or postpone climbing for another day. If risks are low but precipitation still a possibility, carry a lightweight rain jacket, preferably made from a waterproof fabric that breathes. Forgo cotton and carry or wear a polyester-blend mid-layer. In colder climates and at higher altitudes, bring a fleece or wool hat. Balaclavas are great as the eyeholes provide ideal carabiner clip-in points. They can be folded and worn as a beanie, or worn full-length for extra warmth.

If you're near the top of a long route and it begins to rain, your best choice might be to climb on through to the summit. However unpleasant, climbing in the rain is possible (but not recommended for extended periods or after downpours on some types of soft rock). Yet, consider that a rope loses significant strength and stretch capabilities when soaked, and although dry-treated ropes prolong absorption, most treatments wear off. In prolonged or extreme cold, unprotected hands lose dexterity and become useless for gripping holds and handling gear. If necessary, use a combination of aid and free climbing techniques (aka *French free* climbing) to get off the route as quickly as possible. Belay your partner up and find temporary shelter until the rain lets up, then descend. If the descent involves technical, Class 3 and 4 scrambling and the rock is still wet, consider roping up and belaying each other down, or rappelling if it's a possibility. On exposed descents, wet, slippery rock has caused many fatal accidents.

A better decision for unprepared climbers or those farther from the summit is retreat to the nearest escape route or the ground via rappel. The reduced strength of a wet rope is not as crucial on a static rappel as it is for a potential lead fall. You're in luck if the route has fixed anchors from which to rappel, especially if you have two ropes. If not, you'll have to sacrifice a lot of gear for anchors. When it comes to your life, don't be a cheapskate: never trust a single piece or old webbing. Though some climbers trust a single rap ring when rappelling, I prefer an additional backup. Yet, if you're being lowered, never, *ever* thread the rope directly through slings or runners; the moving rope can saw right through the webbing. If necessary, leave two reversed and opposed carabiners.

If it appears the rain might let up, and you're prepared with rainwear and a dry rope in good condition, another option is to hunker down in the most protected area available, wait out the storm, and continue to the top when conditions improve. Just beware of wishful thinking.

Lightning

Lightning kills more people in the US every year than almost all other natural disasters combined. Most of those hit by lightning are either working or playing outdoors. Injuries caused by lightning strikes are also common, ranging from mild to severe. Most serious lightning-related injuries involve cardiac or respiratory arrest caused when the brain "shorts out" from the electrical charge. The good news is that 80% of all pulseless, breathless, lightning victims are resuscitated with CPR when it's performed correctly, so keep your skills sharpened.

Avoid lightning-prone areas when storms are likely. In general, be down and off a summit before early afternoon whenever possible. If weather reports indicate the area is in the middle of a cycle in which storms occur regularly each day, reschedule your long climb in favor of a morning bouldering session or some single-pitch routes.

Otherwise, begin your route in the pre-dawn hours armed with rainwear and an extra rope.

If you are caught in a thunderstorm, thoughtful positioning can reduce your susceptibility to being struck by lightning. Electricity travels most efficiently in terrain offering courses of less resistance. Obvious potential targets are positioned in wide-open spaces. Water is an excellent conductor of electricity and, unfortunately for climbers, so is metal. The most dangerous location for climbers during thunderstorms is on an exposed ridge. Another hazardous position is at the base of a crack system or an exposed face, since this terrain quickly turns into a water course through which electricity easily travels. Because broken terrain and talus stymies the efficiency of electric flow, these locations are preferable.

While your alternatives may be limited if you are mid-climb, by acting quickly you may have time to reposition yourself in a less dangerous location. Heed the first sound of distant thunder and count the seconds between it and the lightning crack to determine its proximity. (Yes, the old one-one-thousand, two-one-thousand count is effective in determining how far away lightning is striking. This rule of thumb roughly equates one second of time with one mile.) Take as many of the following precautions as you can until the lightning has passed:

• Make yourself as small as possible by assuming the lightning-protection position—squat or sit, head down, with knees drawn up to your chest and both arms wrapped around your knees.

• Huddle in a dry, deep cave—crouch in the middle without leaning back against its walls (keep your contact with the rock as limited as possible). Avoid small, wet caves.

• Sit on the non-conductive closed-cell foam pad on your pack (if it has one). Otherwise, sit on your coiled rope.

• Move away from your partner and your climbing hardware.

If you're hiking along the approach or descent and lightning occurs, temporarily abandon your hardware, move away from your partner(s), and huddle in broken terrain such as a large talus field, or in a flat forested area. Avoid open areas such as alpine meadows or large bodies of water, and towering, isolated objects such as lone trees or snags.

Rockfall

Rockfall occurs on single or multipitch routes alike and can be attributed to various factors. Natural rockfall is commonly caused by snow and ice melt—particularly in spring—but can result from animal activity. Probably the most frequent rockfall occurs because of climbers above you. And falling gear can be as hazardous as rock-fall.

Although a climbing helmet can reduce the impact of falling objects, it can't completely eliminate the possibility of harm. Many people won't climb a multiple-pitch route if other climbers are already on it. Other prevention tips include: avoid routes on warm spring days with snow still present in cracks, on ledges, or on the summit; find overhangs and sheltered locations for belay stances; and rise early, so that your party is first in line at the base of popular long climbs.

Prevent rockfall onto others by testing each hold before committing to it completely. Move cautiously across ledges strewn with loose rock, dirt, and gravel, and place directionals to guide the rope away from such terrain. Even a tiny falling pebble, once it accelerates, could injure or kill someone below.

High-Altitude Illnesses

Although physiological changes from increased altitude (barometric pressure) begin occurring as low as 4000' (1250m), most altitude-related illnesses affect people above 8000' (2500m). Generally the higher you go, the more serious the effects. Unfortunately, science has yet to determine what makes one person more susceptible to an altitude-related illness than another. Fitness doesn't even play a role; people in better physical shape may actually be more susceptible because they tend to climb faster.

Acute mountain sickness (*AMS*) is the most common form of altitude sickness and tends to occur six-seventy-two hours after high-altitude exposure. Symptoms of mild-to-moderate AMS include headache, loss of appetite, nausea, insomnia, fatigue, and shortness of breath (relieved immediately with rest). Not a life-threatening condition, AMS can be relieved with rest combined with light exercise.

If AMS symptoms are accompanied by a staggering gait (ataxia), they may indicate a progression toward life-threatening High-Altitude Pulmonary Edema (**HAPE**) and/or High-Altitude Cerebral Edema (**HACE**). If you're not sure, have your partner stand steadily with feet together on level ground. If he or she cannot do this for 10 seconds without shifting a foot, start descending. Symptoms of HAPE include: all those for AMS except that shortness of breath is not relieved with rest; a cough producing a pink, frothy mucous; chest pain; increased heart rate; and crackling or gurgling sounds with breathing. HACE symptoms include severe headache, extreme ataxia, and personality changes progressing to disorientation and combative behavior. While both HACE and HAPE can occur simultaneously, HAPE tends to come on gradually while HACE is rapid. Climbers with ataxia, or HACE or HAPE symptoms, *must descend immediately*, as these conditions are life-threatening and will not resolve at altitude. Neither of these conditions are common below 14,000' (4375m), particularly HACE. Nevertheless, if you're prepared to identify either condition, you may be able to save a life.

To prevent altitude-related illnesses, climbers should stay hydrated, drinking enough water to keep urine clear. In addition, climbers should gradually acclimatize before climbing at elevations significantly higher than where they reside. For instance, if you're at sea level and ascending about 14,000' (4375m) to climb Mt. Whitney in the Sierra Nevada, consider arriving three or four days early to acclimatize. Above 10,000' (3125m), the Wilderness Medicine Institute (WMI) recommends you gain no more altitude than 1000' (312m) per 24 hours. If this isn't possible, know the signs of HAPE and HACE and be prepared to descend should they appear. Diamox (acetazolamide) is a prescription medication used as a prophylactic against AMS, which can also reduce symptoms from severe to mild. Because Diamox is a diuretic, be prepared for excessive urination and drink a lot of water.

Interestingly enough, since altitude illnesses don't develop within the first six hours of reaching higher altitudes, an extremely fast team able to approach, climb, and descend a route within this period can actually avoid altitude-related illnesses altogether. Buck Tilton of WMI, author of several texts on wilderness medicine, cautions, "This does not exclude the possibility of unusual breathlessness and fatigue or the possibility of a debilitating injury that prevents the descent." As a new leader you should save such a timeframe for a short route with a simple approach and an easy descent.

THE DESCENT

Descents from long routes involve walk-offs and/or rappels. The complexity and danger factor of a descent is measured in terms of length and terrain. For instance, two short rappels down a loose gully with several hundred feet of Class 3 scrambling might be far more dangerous than 10 rappels down the ascent line of a clean, steep route. Climbers must stay alert and resist the urge to relax simply because the summit has been attained. Ringing especially true for the multipitch descent is the adage, *It's not over until it's over*.

Multipitch Rappelling

As long as you stay focused on multiple rappels, and follow the guidelines listed in Chapter 4, the following suggestions will help keep you free of epics:

• After each rappel clip into the next rappel anchor with your daisy chain or cow's tail before removing your device from the rope.

• If you're last to rappel, don't let go of the lines after clipping into the next anchor and disengaging your device.

• Make sure at least one rope end is threaded through rap rings at each intermediate rappel station before pulling your lines. Continue threading the rope as you retrieve them and, when both ends come down, the rope(s) will be almost ready for the next rappel. Make any small adjustments as needed to keep the center point or knot at masterpoint level.

• In windy conditions don't lose control of your rope(s). If necessary, consider lowering the first person in line to rappel, and have him or her tie in the loose ends at the anchor below before you follow on rappel.

• If you're exhausted or injured, have your partner rappel first and give you a "fireman's belay" from below. This simply involves the "belayer" holding both lines loosely, but pulling tightly to halt the rappeller's progress should he or she lose control.

• As suggested in Chapter 4, check and double-check all primary links, tie knots on the ends of each rappel line, and use a friction hitch backup.

Class 3 & 4 Terrain

Trad climbers often forgo ropes and protection when scrambling on Class 3 and 4 terrain (see Chapter 8), though a slip can be fatal. While seasoned mountaineers have little trouble covering such ground, climbers without much backcountry experience can have difficulties, particularly if tired from a long climb. Without honed backcountry skills, don't attempt Class 3 and 4 descents after nightfall, and be prepared to rope up on uncomfortably exposed or loose sections. Absorb advice from your resources before the climb, and bring any available maps. Until you're walking safely on a well-maintained trail, stay alert.

Scree & Talus

Scree are tiny shards of rock and dirt covering slopes of varying degrees of steepness in backcountry settings. Ranging from bread-box to VW size, talus consist of larger versions of scree. Scree and talus slopes can result from glacial debris in moraines, or from long-term erosion or rockfall.

Wear your helmet when climbing or descending these slopes. Be careful not to dislodge loose rock, and avoid traveling directly above or below your partner in case you do. How long ago the debris was deposited determines the stability of a talus slope; if recent, it will

Potential Problems & Solutions on Multipitch Rappels

There are many issues that can arise on rappel, particularly in multiple rappels. Some common problems with their solutions are provided below:

• **You have accidentally passed the next rappel anchor and are now below it.** Ascend the lines using friction hitches (see Chapter 7) to reach the stance. Be sure to wrap each cord around both rope strands. With moderate terrain, climbing might be a possibility, as long as you slide a friction hitch up the rope strands with each move.

• **You drop your rappel device.** If you're carrying at least four standard D or oval carabiners (better), you can set up a carabiner brake system (see Chapter 8). Otherwise have your partner tie them onto one end of the rope and you can haul them up.

• **You've just completed a slightly traversing rappel, with several more to go before reaching the ground. When your partner joins you at the stance, he or she disengages the rope from the device and lets go of both ends. You watch helplessly as the rope lines fly across the rock face and stop several feet (or more) from your reach.** Ask for assistance from parties (if present) rappelling above you. Or get creative: extend a chain of gear to reach the rope end you need to pull (either end if you're using a single rope). Athletic tape might help you join the gear. Use longer rigid yet fairly light pieces such as nut tools and wired Stoppers. If you're on a ledge, look for useful sticks and branches. Now, extend your tie-in point to the anchor with cordelettes and/or several girth-hitched slings, and move out onto the face closest to the ropes and reach.... Good luck!

• **Upon attempted retrieval the rope becomes stuck; no amount of pulling will disengage it.** If you have access to both rope ends, and the rope is still threaded through the anchors, create friction knots to ascend (Note: Each prusik loop must be wrapped around both rope strands—see Chapter 7). Disengage the stuck line when you reach it, then rappel back down. With only one line available, don't think you'll ascend the rope hand over hand up the fixed line without a belay. After considering your fate if the rope shimmies loose and/or you fall, tie in and get a belay. If you're lucky, the terrain is moderate and you'll have enough rope available to lead up (belayed) and free the stuck line. If not, combine aid moves with free moves to ascend. Without enough rope to do this you're in trouble, if you haven't reached the ground.

be very loose. When you descend over steep scree, take deliberate steps, letting yourself slide a bit. With hesitant, unsure steps the going is slower and probably more harrowing. Relax and get a rhythm going, but, if you're too worried, ask your partner for a belay.

Snow & Ice

In mountain environments snow and ice travel on approaches and descents might require the use of an ice ax. If you're bringing one, know how to use it. Practice self-arrest beforehand with an experienced guide or mentor on high-angle snow patches with long runouts. For crossing short sections of snow or ice, you could share one ax between two partners. The lead can chop footholds for the second, and then send the ax down to the second for his or her ascent. If you forgo an ax but come upon unexpected snow or ice, substitute two hand-sized sharp rocks.

In late spring when you're crossing large talus covered in snow, travel early in the day when the snow is frozen and still relatively solid. Under softer conditions you're at high risk for breaking through boulder gaps and incurring a significant injury.

If an approach or descent involves extensive glacier travel, be familiar with the basics of moving over such terrain, including coping with *bergschrunds*, *seracs*, *crevasse* rescue, avalanche danger, and other alpine hazards. If you're not, choose a route with an easier approach or descent, take a basic mountaineering course, or learn these skills from an experienced mentor.

Epics

"The adventure you seek isn't always the adventure you get."

—*Unknown*

Every longtime trad climber has a good tale about a climbing foray turned epic. Sharing misfortunes increases climbers' awareness of their own vulnerability. But don't bolster your own ego by critiquing an accident of another climber: it could have been you. Understand what went wrong and when, and use this information to prevent mistakes of your own.

An epic often results from one poor decision or careless action. Getting a late start, not bringing enough water, climbing off-route, climbing regardless of threatening weather, dropping critical gear, discovering the route is too difficult for the team's collective ability, getting a rope stuck—these are all grist for the epic mill and all preventable. Regardless of best intentions and preparations, though, epics occur. Once a mistake is made, do whatever you can to prevent the situation from worsening. Every epic has a turning point when you can either resolve it safely through teamwork, or it balloons into a serious accident. When facing the consequences of an error, gather your respective wits before the situation spirals out of control.

Retreat

Just as noteworthy as summiting is making the difficult decision to retreat. In my opinion, success has more to do with style and staying alive than reaching the top. Facing climbing peers after a retreat, and coping with feelings of failure, can take more courage than undergoing dangerous maneuvers in poor style to reach the top. Having said that, go with your gut feeling about retreat, without letting your ego interfere.

THE UNPLANNED BIVOUAC

Though an unplanned *bivouac* is uncomfortable at best and utter misery at worst, if, having summitted, you doubt your ability to descend—either because of imminent darkness or other changing conditions (such as a snowfield refreezing)—wait until morning. Lightweight items that make an unplanned "bivy" more tolerable include:

• **Fire Starters**—a lighter or matches (preferably waterproof) and kindling material such as steel wool, a small amount of paper, or a few cotton balls previously soaked in Vasoline (petroleum jelly);

• **Extra Clothing**—wool or fleece hat (or balaclava), wool- or polyester-blend socks, a fleece pullover; and a wind/rain jacket; and

Mike Pennings Collection

Retreat Factors

Climber: Mike Pennings
Years Trad Free Climbing: 18
Average Trad Lead Ability: 5.12-
Favorite Trad Climbing Area(s):
BlackCanyon (Colorado)
& Patagonia
Most Respected Trad Free Climber:
Charlie Porter

The little voice inside me says when to throw in the towel on an ascent—no formula governs when to retreat and when to push farther. My decision is affected by weather conditions, route conditions, difficulty of the climb ahead, time of day, partner psyche and desire, personal psyche and desire, other climbers on the route, when my wife expects me home, etc. Yet the most important factor influencing the decision is intuition.

Jeff Hollenbaugh and I went to the Kitchatnas in Alaska to attempt the first ascent of the southeast face of Mt. Nevermore. An ava-lanche that occurred near the base of the route buried a haul bag containing most of our gear. Approaching the wall to search for the lost bag, we both experienced an eerie feeling—the mountain didn't want us to be there. Without a very thorough search—despite our pilot not returning for three and a half weeks—we abandoned our effort.

In a situation where you want to climb but your partner wants to retreat, you must respect your partner's reasons. Whether they're just being lazy or truly believe they'll die if they continue isn't really for you to decide. By continuing upward with a begrudging partner, you potentially compromise the safety of both team members.

—Mike Pennings

• **SPACE**™ **Emergency Blanket**—super lightweight Mylar "blanket" that retains 80% radiated body heat.

Build a fire in a contained space if you can find dry timber, and try to keep it burning through the night. Use extreme caution to prevent it getting out of control and clean up properly in the morning (see "Leave No Trace," in Chapter 8). Assume the heat-saving fetal position and stay close to your partner to help keep each other warm. Use the rope and pack (or leaves and pine needles) as insulation from the cold ground. A removable closed-cell pad that forms the back panel of some packs makes excellent insulation. In addition, extension flaps at the mouth can transform your pack into a waist-high bivy bag. If it begins to rain or snow, seek shelter under an overhang or in a cave. Some outdoor enthusiasts carry extra-large plastic garbage bags for such a situation—not a bad idea considering how little they weigh.

What if I don't make it to the summit? Don't wait until the last minute to find a good bivy ledge. As twilight fades, many deluded teams forge ahead frantically, passing spacious ledges that would soften the blow of an unplanned bivy. When halted by complete darkness, these climbers often have no other option but to endure the night dangling from the anchors of a hanging belay. If you can't locate a ledge, situate yourself under an overhang, if possible. If the weather is threatening, avoid perches at the base of obvious water paths (grooves, crack systems, black streaks).

Certainly not for everyone, the multipitch trad adventure does offer memorable experiences. If you have this longing, you could get yourself hooked—it happens. If it does to you, stay safe by maintaining realistic goals, partnering with competent people, and never shedding your Beginner's Mind. Also take responsibility for the risks you shoulder by learning self-rescue skills, and encourage your regular partners to do the same. Basic self-rescue techniques are discussed in the next chapter.

Chapter 7

Introduction to Self-Rescue

Heidi Pestetrfield

The climbing experience can often seem like an amusement park ride in which thrills are safely guaranteed. Each successful and safe ascent reinforces this illusion until one day an injury or mishap harshly dispels your false sense of invulnerability. There are no guarantees in trad climbing; you work toward reducing risks but can never eliminate them. Since routes typically lure climbers to heights well above the possibility of a simple retreat, knowing how to extricate your team from a mishap is essential. "Self-rescue" refers broadly to taking responsibility for your team without relying on outside help; it is a specific elaboration of self-reliance. By studying and practicing self-rescue skills and techniques, you prepare yourself for action should your team's "what ifs" become all too real.

After prevention, self-rescue skills are your best insurance against rescuers having to pluck you from a wall when you run into trouble. Outside assistance can be costly and undependable. In remote areas, professional rescues are often unavailable. In regions where they are, you might have to pick up the tab for your rescue or, worse, find your team at the mercy of an incompetent rescue crew. Although climbing areas such as Yosemite National Park rely on a well-trained Search and Rescue

(SAR) team, others may not. Your rescue may fall into the hands of a group of well-meaning but inexperienced sheriff deputies generally better equipped to fight crime than perform high-angle rescue.

Complex self-rescue scenarios can require techniques, materials, and/or skills beyond the scope of this book, but this chapter introduces the basics. Hands-on practice is indispensable when learning and the only realistic way to understand basic concepts. Don't try to learn these skills solely from reading this or any other book or article. Taking a class will help. Contact your local guide service to enroll in one. You can prepare yourself for the class and improve your level of understanding by studying this chapter before and after. Once you receive professional instruction, begin practicing these techniques in low-risk settings. As your leading skills increase, add techniques to your repertoire, learn how to use varied tools, and share what you've learned with fellow climbers.

A clear head is essential for safe and successful self-rescue. In his book, *Self-Rescue*, David Fasulo says, "The most important tool in any self-rescue is your brain. Carefully survey the scene to prevent further difficulties and ensure safety. Plan your course of action safely, and if necessary locate assistance."[11]

At first, self-rescue techniques may seem very complex, yet most operations really only combine a few, fundamental techniques. With your mind open, absorb the information in small doses and practice a lot. Once these fundamentals become second nature, your self-sufficiency on the rock is within sight.

PREVENTION & RESPONSIBILITY

Most trad climbers now racking up mileage on long technical routes know little about self-rescue. Because confidence soars with success, these climbers sometimes get stricken with a case of *It can't happen to me,* or *If it happens to me, I'll figure it out on the spot.* Winging it may be possible for a longtime climber with keen tech skills, but is wishful thinking for most. Learning self-rescue empowers you to take full responsibility of every aspect of your adventure, epics notwithstanding.

Self-rescue is less likely to be necessary if you use sound judgment to prevent errors. Climb within your honest ability level and make realistic choices in regard to route length, weather, and daylight. Analyze the mistakes of other climbers. Don't feel badly about discussing their accidents; a real-life close call of someone you know is highly affecting, and you can really learn from the mistakes. Valuable insight can also be gained from reading. Check out the American Alpine Club's annual *Accidents in North American Mountaineering*, as well as my personal favorite, *Close Calls* by John Long (illustrated by Tami Knight).

FIRST AID

All climbers should know basic first aid and Cardiopulmonary Resuscitation (CPR). If you're climbing in backcountry settings, advanced first-aid skills are highly recommended. If, while climbing in a remote area, your partner hits his or her head during a leader fall, could you distinguish a minor goose-egg from a head injury that requires immediate evacuation? Could you monitor your partner for signs of increasing intracranial pressure that is life threatening? If your partner dislocates a shoulder or wrist, what would you do? Using what you have on hand, could you splint a fractured bone to stabilize an injured partner for evacuation? For climbers who frequently venture into remote areas, a Wilderness First Responder (WFR) certification provides a very comprehensive set of lay medical skills. A WFR course prepares you to distinguish between conditions that require immediate evacuation and those that do not. Curriculum includes how to treat, stabilize, and evacuate victims using improvised equipment. WFR courses address the scenarios and conditions mentioned above, as well as numerous others, including: wound management, hypothermia, altitude illness, heat exhaustion and heat stroke, frostbite, dehydration, shock, and lightning injuries. Ten-day trainings are held throughout the US and in some locations abroad. Locate companies offering WFR courses in your area by searching the Internet.

A victim's physical and mental condition plays a large role in determining which method of self-rescue you employ. For instance, if a climber has sustained serious injuries, lowering or raising might compound them. In this case, you may have to ascend or descend to the victim first, assess his or her condition and provide assistance, and then perform an assisted rappel. The severity of your partner's injuries might also determine whether you can safely execute all or part of the rescue without outside assistance.

Conditions posing an immediate threat to life take priority over rescue efforts. Always initiate first aid if your partner isn't breathing, doesn't have a pulse, is bleeding, has a potential cervical spine injury, or is exposed to environmental hazards (rockfall, extreme heat or cold, etc.). Learning to conduct a primary survey of the victim's condition allows you to identify and treat immediate threats to life. This skill is taught thoroughly in WFR and other first-aid courses, while CPR courses cover the basics.

EQUIPMENT

The following equipment composes a basic kit for performing the introductory self-rescue techniques outlined in this chapter:

• A cordelette reserved specifically for rescue scenarios;

• Two locking carabiners (two reversed and opposed standard 'biners can be substituted for each but are awkward to use in some applications);

• Four standard carabiners;

• 4' (1.25m) of 6mm accessory cord cut and tied into two 12" (30cm) loops with 4" (10cm) tails[12]; and

• Three ⁹⁄₁₆" (1.4cm) shoulder-length runners made from nylon webbing (not Spectra).

While you're gaining lead climbing experience, carry these items with you every time you rope up, and don't hand them over to the leader at changeovers on multipitch routes. With greater experience you can explore alternate self-rescue methods that enable one material or tool to be substituted for another. For an excellent resource on such methods, see Fasulo's *Self-Rescue* listed in the Resources section.

KNOTS & HITCHES

Knowing a handful of knots and hitches will prepare you for learning the self-rescue methods described in this chapter. Use the mule knot to lock off the belay and free up your hands as rescuer, and the *Munter mule knot* to let you release a knot under tension and transfer loads. Friction hitches grip the rope. Besides serving as brakeline backups, you can use them to transfer loads and ascend fixed ropes.

Friction Hitches

The *prusik* is the most common of many friction hitches, all of which possess the capacity to slide up or down a rope when unweighted, yet grip it under load. Some other friction hitches include the *Klemheist*, the *Bachman*, and the *autoblock*. Prusik and autoblock friction hitches are described here.

Most friction hitches (with the exception of the prusik) can be tied with either an accessory cord a or 9⁄16″ (1.4cm) tubular nylon sling. Do not use slings made from Spectra or Dyneema. Cord that is 6mm in diameter is ideal for use with the average 9.4-10.5mm climbing rope. For use on ropes of lesser diameter, use 5mm cord. Cord smaller than 5mm is too weak, and larger than 6mm won't grip. Since any hitch with too few wraps can slip on loaded ropes and burn from friction heat, always test each hitch prior to use. If it slips, add more wraps.

Prusik *(Photos: 1-3, opposite page, left side)*
The prusik works effectively only with cord, but unlike other friction hitches, you can tie it easily with one hand— a huge benefit in some scenarios. It is multidirectional

Prusik

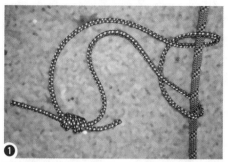

Prusik hitch start (a loose girth hitch) on a 10mm rope

Wrapped twice

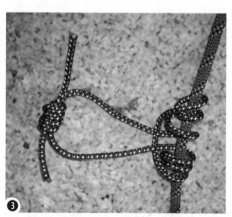

One final wrap (3 total) and the weighted prusik will "bite" the rope. (Add another wrap for added friction if desired or necessary for smaller diameter ropes.)

Autoblock

To tie an autoblock on a 10mm line, wrap your cord or webbing three or four times around the rope.

Complete by clipping both loop ends to your carabiner.

(able to hold loads from either end), but difficult to loosen after being loaded. To tie a prusik, make a girth hitch (see Chapter 8) around the rope. Keep this initial hitch loose and tie two to three more girth hitches with the free loop, adding each new wrap to the center. Three loops are usually sufficient to get the hitch to "bite" the rope.

Autoblock (aka French Prusik)
(Photos: 1, 2, page 171, right side)
Also multidirectional, the autoblock releases with relative ease after being loaded. Because of this, it works great both as a brake-line backup for rappelling (see Chapter 4), and for ascending a fixed line. Another advantage over the prusik is that it can be tied with either cord or non-Spectra webbing. A drawback is that it's difficult to tie with one hand. To tie an autoblock, wrap your loop of cord or webbing candy-cane fashion at least four times around the rope. Complete the hitch by clipping both loop ends to a locking carabiner.

Basic Mule Knot *(Illustration: opposite page)*
Use the basic mule knot to tie off a loaded belay rope and free your hands, the first step in escaping the belay. Use it also in combination with the Munter hitch to transfer loads (see Munter mule and Belay Escape).

Say you have caught a fall, are holding your partner on tension, and want to free your hands to begin a self-rescue task. If you are braking with your right hand[13], take a fairly large loop of your brake line (the non-loaded strand) and feed it through the locking carabiner from right to left. Feed a bight of slack from this loop *under* the loaded rope from left to right, and make a twist (clockwise) in the rope. Using a bight from the remaining loose portion of the loop, form another coil to the left of the loaded strand with another twist (counterclockwise). Feed the left coil through the right coil over the loaded rope strand. Tighten and cinch the knot closely to your device. With the protruding bight, tie an overhand knot to the loaded strand. For extra security, clip a standard carabiner to the final tail. **(Note: It is absolutely essential to complete the mule knot with an overhand; all subsequent references to the mule knot assume it.)**

Basic Mule Knot

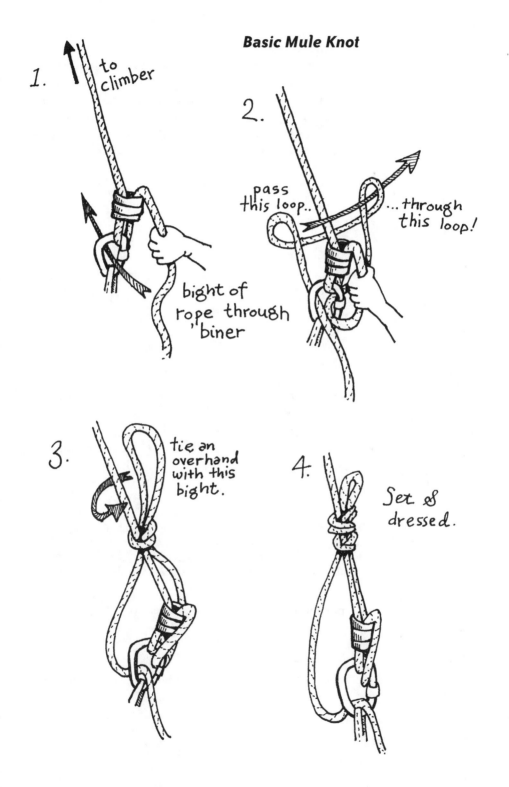

1. to climber

bight of rope through 'biner

2. pass this loop.. ...through this loop!

3. tie an overhand with this bight.

4. Set & dressed.

Munter Mule *(Illustration: below)*

The Munter mule is a combination of a Munter hitch and a mule knot. Because this knot can be easily released when weighted, it is ideal for transferring loads in self-rescue scenarios. Tie a Munter hitch onto a locking carabiner, then tie a mule knot as described previously, but without passing a loop through the locking carabiner.

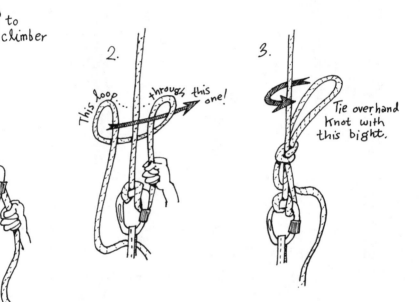

1. to climber

use this slack to tie mule

2. This loop ... ... through this one!

3. Tie overhand knot with this bight.

This illustration depicts the Munter mule tied with a *single* strand of climbing rope—an application used to free your hands when belaying with a Munter hitch. In some applications, however, you will tie the Munter mule with your cordelette loop, so the strands you are working with are *doubled*.

FUNDAMENTAL TECHNIQUES

Self-rescue scenarios can vary from simple to complex, but no matter whether you're assisting an immobilized leader or helping your second pass a difficult section on a route beyond his/her capabilities, you'll use one or a combination of four basic techniques: **rope ascent, belay escape, assisted raise,** and/or **assisted descent**.

Don't attempt any technique presented here without first practicing it in a low-risk setting under the watchful eye of an experienced mentor. These methods require an absolutely reliable anchor, as most result in a tremendous multiplication of forces. It is a good idea to reinforce your belay anchor before proceeding. Backing up your work is also important, especially during training. Create a backup with a figure-eight on a bight clipped to your anchor. Also, remember to use locking carabiners (or two reversed and opposed standard 'biners) on all your backups and primary links.

Rope Ascent (Illustration: following page)

The rope ascent is the most basic of all self-rescue skills. The following outlines the "Texas style" method:

Step 1: Attach a friction hitch to the taut rope. Using a locking carabiner, connect yourself with the appropriate-length sling (no more than the distance between your waist and forehead when standing).

Step 2: Add a second friction hitch to the rope below the first one. Make a foot sling for this hitch by attaching either two slings girthed together or one long sling (measuring no more than the distance between your feet and waist when standing). Different body types may require fine tuning of the sling length. Your cordelette can be used in lieu of the sling(s).

Step 3: Alternately weight each hitch to ascend, making progress by sliding the unweighted hitch up the rope. Begin by standing up in the lower loop. Without weighting the upper loop, push it up the rope as high as possible. Now weight it and, reaching down, slide the lower hitch up the rope until it is near the upper one.

Step 4: Repeat Step 3 until you have reached your destination, tying backup figure-eights into a large lock-

1.

Rope Ascent

Weight lower friction hitch by standing up on this leg . . .

2.

. . . slide upper friction hitch up as high as possible . . .

3.

. . . hang by upper hitch while you slide the lower hitch up, then repeat the process!

ing carabiner attached to your harness every 15 feet (more often above ledges or close to the ground). For an additional backup, link the lower hitch to your harness loosely with a long sling. (Note: for clarity, backup is not shown in illustration.)

Tips

• Ascending a fixed rope can be strenuous, especially on overhanging terrain. Make sure you fully weight the upper loop at each opportunity, as this is your only chance to rest. Bend one leg and tuck it under your torso, resting your butt on the heel of your foot; you can stretch the other out straight in front of you.

• For optimal efficiency, adjust the slings to a length that minimizes effort and maximizes the distance you can cover with each slide. If your upper sling is too short, progress will be slow and you'll tire faster. If it is too long, you'll find it difficult to rest and won't maximize the potential distance you'd otherwise cover. Before setting off, try out your system by ascending a short distance. Then take the time to adjust the sling lengths correctly. Reduce a sling's length by tying an overhand knot onto it. This knot simply takes up space thereby shortening the runner.

Common Scenarios

Instances when you need to ascend the rope include, but aren't limited to, the following scenarios:

• After taking a leader fall from above an overhang, you might end up below the ceiling, dangling helplessly in space too far from the rock wall to gain purchase for climbing back. Lowering might not be an option, especially if you have used more than half the rope or the route traverses significantly. Ascending the rope as your belayer maintains tension will get you back to your last piece.

• When seconding a multipitch route, you might encounter a section too difficult for you to free climb. Since lowering to the ground isn't an option and you don't want your lead climber to have to set up an assisted raise, you might ask your partner to lock you off on tension and let you ascend the "fixed" line past the difficult section.

• If you accidentally rappel past an anchor when executing multiple rappels, you might have to ascend two lines together to reach the stance above. Since you attach your friction hitch to both lines, add additional wraps for optimal security. This is also a solution for disengaging a stuck rappel line if your rope is still through the anchors and you have access to both ends (see Chapter 6).

• If you are belaying and the leader takes a fall, becoming immobilized and requiring assistance, you may need to ascend the rope. In this scenario the anchored rope won't let you tie backups. Instead, use a third hitch as a backup (see "Leader Rescue Overview").

Belay Escape (Illustrations: pages 180-181)

Escaping a loaded belay is the first step in many self-rescue efforts. Briefly, it involves freeing your hands and transferring the weight of the loaded rope off your body, so you can disengage from your belay mechanism. This method uses the Munter mule to shift the load first onto a friction hitch so you can disengage your belay device, and then directly onto the anchor. This provides the opportunity to either transfer the load again, or resume belaying. Use this method any time you are belaying off your harness with the rope redirected through the anchor to the climber.

Step 1: Tie a mule knot onto the loaded rope strand to free your hands. Tie a backup on the loose brake line, leaving two arm's length of slack between your device and the anchor.

Step 2: Using a bight of your cordelette, attach a friction hitch onto the taut line leading to the climber, then, with the double strand of the other end of the cordelette, tie a Munter mule on a locking 'biner attached to the anchor. (This Munter mule will let you ease the load onto another Munter mule you tie with the rope in Step 4.)

Step 3: Now transfer the load onto the friction knot by releasing the original mule knot that you tied to free your hands. (You have now officially escaped the belay. The friction knot set-up is backed up by your Step 1 tie-off. The next two steps allow you to transfer the load directly onto the anchors.)

Step 4: Using the brake line between the load and your backup, attach a Munter mule to the anchors with a locking carabiner.

Step 5: Release the mule knot at the Munter mule you tied with the cordelette, then let the Munter slide, transferring the load directly onto the anchor (now secured by the Munter mule you just tied with the rope). To resume belaying, pop the mule knot free and belay off the anchor with the remaining Munter.

Comments

If you are belaying the second directly off the anchor with a Munter hitch, his or her weight is already on the anchor, simplifying the belay escape. All that's required is to tie a mule knot (and back up) to free the hands. This is why rock guides prefer this belay method for clients who are following.

Common Scenarios

Almost all self-rescue attempts require belay escape. Whether you are going to initiate an assisted raise, rescue the leader, or rescue the second via rappelling, a belay escape frees you to take action.

Assisted Raise *(Illustration: right)*

Few climbers—even the strongest—could hoist their partner hand-over-hand on a rope. Raising a climber requires some sort of mechanical-advantage system. The most versatile and widely used raising method in climbing is the *Z-rig*.

The 3:1 Z-rig is an improvised pulley system that provides approximately twice your unassisted strength. (Theoretically the advantage is 3:1, but

Assisted Raise

ANCHOR

MASTER POINT

MUNTER MULE
in
CORDELETTE

the 'Z'

PULL!

FRICTION HITCH

FRICTION HITCH
(RATCHET)

To VICTIM

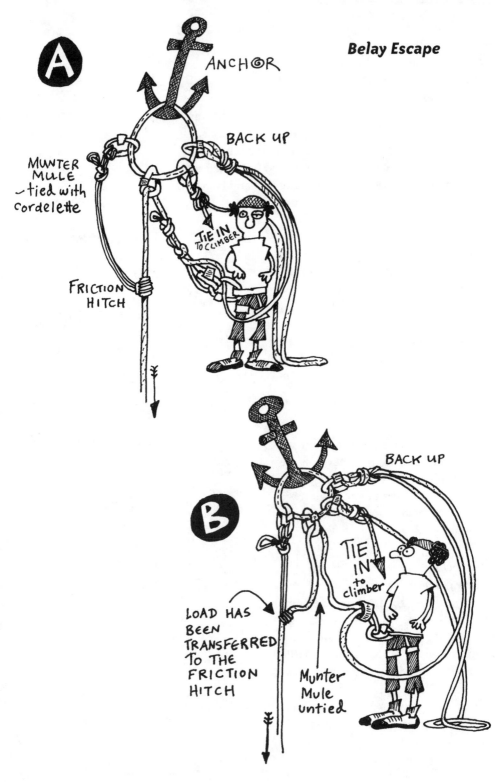

Belay Escape

A ANCHOR

BACK UP

MUNTER MULE ~tied with cordelette

TIE IN TO CLIMBER

FRICTION HITCH

B BACK UP

TIE IN to climber

LOAD HAS BEEN TRANSFERRED TO THE FRICTION HITCH

Munter Mule untied

in practice it ranges from 1½-2, depending on the degree of friction.) It employs two friction hitches: one (the locking or "tractor" hitch) helps you pull rope up, and the other (the ratcheting hitch) prevents back-slippage of the rope pulled up. Once the stretch is out of the rope, for every 3 feet you pull up, the victim will rise 1 foot.

Step 1: Follow Steps 1 through 3 in "Belay Escape" (see page 178). You have now transferred the load to a friction hitch (which will serve as the ratchet for your Z-rig) and to the anchor, via a Munter Mule tied with your cordelette. Your hands are now free to work.

Step 2: Using a short loop of cord or webbing, attach a second friction hitch on the loaded rope above the existing ratchet hitch. This will serve as the locking hitch.

Step 3: Clip a locking carabiner into the anchor, and run the slack side of the rope through this carabiner, and down and through another 'biner attached to the locking (upper) hitch. Now you have your Z.

Step 4: To raise a victim, pull upward on the slack rope until the upper (locking) hitch almost meets the anchor. Now slide the lower (ratchet) hitch back down the rope (toward the victim) and ease the load onto it. Now slide the locking hitch back down and repeat the process. As you make progress, clip backups every 15 feet alternately into two, pre-placed carabiners at the anchor.

Tips & Comments

• The locking hitch can instead be established below the ratchet instead of above it. This allows hauling in longer increments, but requires careful monitoring of the ratchet to prevent it from slipping through the locking carabiner at the anchor.

• A Z-rig assisted raise requires the victim to remove lead protection, or at least unclip the rope from protection. If the victim is unable to do this, you must rappel down to provide assistance.

• Even though mechanical advantages help make raising a climber easier, it is still a difficult and strenuous procedure. Excess friction in the system (e.g., raising a victim up low-angle terrain) makes the process even more difficult. Before launching into an extended Z-rig raise, consider other options. If you have enough rope and your partner will likely be able to continue, rappel down to him or her, establish another anchor, and perform an assisted rappel to the ground.

Common Scenarios

Trad free climbing scenarios requiring the use of an assisted raise include but aren't limited to the following:

• The second can't get past a difficult section and doesn't know how to ascend the rope.

• The second, though conscious enough to unclip or clean protection, has been injured and is unable to physically or mentally make the moves required to reach the belay.

• The second, having fallen on an unprotected traverse, is now off-route and dangling in space too far from the rock to climb again. He or she is not carrying the equipment necessary to ascend the rope.

Assisted Descent

If your partner's condition is such that he or she is incapable of rappelling solo or being lowered, the simplest descent option is the *tandem rappel*. The description below assumes that both climbers are clipped into a secure and reliable anchor with a daisy chain or cow's tail before beginning. It also assumes you have tied a safety knot in appropriate rope end(s) to prevent rappelling off the end of the rope.

Tandem Rappel *(Illustration: following page)*

Two climbers descend on the same rope, attached to the same device, with one partner in command of braking. First, prepare the rope(s) in the same manner as with any standard rappel (see Chapter 4).

Step 1: Thread the descent rope into a rappel device attached to a locking carabiner. Girth-hitch a single-length runner to your harness and a double-length to the victim's. Clip both into the locker.

Step 2: Take control of the brake line, assemble a backup friction hitch attached to your leg loops, and descend with your partner.

Common Scenarios

Instances when you use the tandem rappel include but aren't limited to the following scenarios:

• When beginners experience severe apprehension over an impending rappel descent;

• When at any time during a descent you suspect your partner's consciousness level is deteriorating, due to extreme fatigue, altitude illness, hypothermia, or heat stroke/exhaustion;

• When rescuing the leader (note: Learning the more advanced *counterweight rappel* simplifies the leader-rescue procedure; though beyond the scope of this book, I recommend the counterweight method of assisted descent for intermediate self-rescue students).

Tandem Rappel

brake hand

autoblock
backup
to harness

Passing a Knot

If you are fortunate enough to have two ropes, you can sometimes tie them together to reach to the ground faster, either via standard rappelling or lowering. One drawback of this tactic is that you'll need to get past the knot joining the ropes together. The two methods described below require advance rigging.

Rappel Knot Pass *(Illustrations: following page)*

Step 1: Pre-rig a friction hitch above the rappel device and clip it into your rappel/belay loop on your harness. Keep the hitch loose through your initial descent and make sure it doesn't get sucked into your rappel device. I suggest you use the autoblock because of all the friction hitches it is the most easily released when weighted.

Step 2: Rappel until you approach the knot, then engage the hitch when it is within an arm's length of the knot. Now your device is unweighted.

Step 3: 3-4 feet below the knot joining the ropes, tie a backup figure-eight and clip it to your harness with a locking carabiner.

Step 4: Remove your rappel device and reattach it below the knot.

Step 5: Establish a rapell backup below your device.

Step 6: Now loosen the friction hitch and transfer your weight from the upper hitch back to your rappel device. Finally, untie the figure-eight backup.

Comments: On overhanging terrain, it may be difficult or impossible to loosen and remove the loaded hitch (step 6). If this is the case, you must first un-weight the hitch. To do this, two options exist:

A. Loop a section of the unloaded rope strand around one foot, then, grasping a bight of the rope taut at your chest, stand up and loosen the now un-weighted hitch with your other hand.

B. Attach another friction hitch onto the loaded rope and extend (with girthed runners) a loop of webbing into which you can stand to un-weight the hitch, and then loosen and remove it. (See lower illustraion on next page.)

Rappel Knot Pass

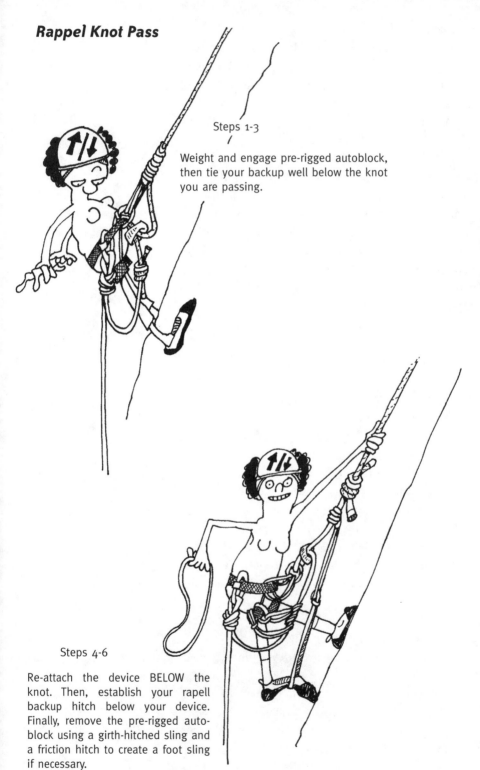

Steps 1-3

Weight and engage pre-rigged autoblock, then tie your backup well below the knot you are passing.

Steps 4-6

Re-attach the device BELOW the knot. Then, establish your rapell backup hitch below your device. Finally, remove the pre-rigged auto-block using a girth-hitched sling and a friction hitch to create a foot sling if necessary.

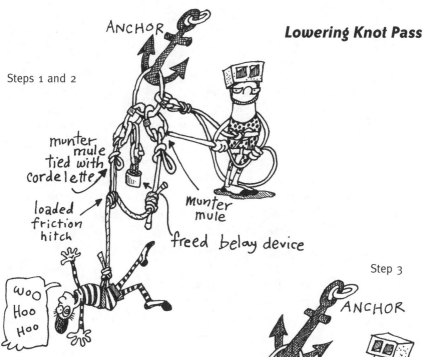

ANCHOR

Lowering Knot Pass

Steps 1 and 2

munter mule tied with cordelette

loaded friction hitch

Munter mule

freed belay device

WOO Hoo Hoo

Step 3

ANCHOR

Knot is passed now.

Lowering Knot Pass

(Illustration: this page)

Pre-rig your system as follows: with your cordelette, tie a friction hitch on the rope strand to be loaded, and attach it to the anchor with a Munter mule (same procedure as Step 2 of "Belay Escape," page 178.) Opposite the knot joining the two ropes, use the rope to tie a Munter mule directly onto a locking carabiner attached to the anchor.

Before you begin lowering the victim, consider the overall picture—to pass the knot, you've got to release your initial belay/lowering device. Engaging the hitch when you reach the knot will allow you to do this. Next you need to transfer the load from the hitch to the Munter mule on the second rope (opposite the knot), so you can continue lowering. You can make this initial transition because the Munter mule tied with the cordelette can be released under load, and you can ease the load onto the second rope with the remaining Munter on the cordelette. Releasing the mule knot on the second rope leaves a Munter for continued lowering.

Step 1: Lower the victim with your belay/lowering device, tending the pre-rigged friction hitch so it won't bind. Just before the knot reaches the device, allow the hitch to load, then remove your device. (Note: the pre-rigged Munter mule tied with the rope is your backup.)

Step 2: Release the Munter mule on the loaded friction hitch, keeping control of the free end of the cordelette. Let the Munter slide, transferring the load onto the second rope below the knot.

Step 3: Establish control of the brake line, and then release the mule knot tied with the rope. With your other hand, remove the friction hitch from the rope so it won't snag later on the rock. Continue lowering with the remaining Munter.

LEADER RESCUE OVERVIEW

Rescuing the leader is complex, often risky, and requires thorough knowledge of the aforementioned techniques. As with other self-rescue methods—but more emphatically with the leader rescue—don't attempt it for the first time on the fly. Practice it beforehand in a class, then later in a low-risk, controlled setting with a top-rope backup.

The steps described below assume a scenario where the pitch is fairly direct (without major traverses), and that you have adequate rope available for the descent. They also assume you have only one rope, and have confirmed the reliability of the high piece anchoring the victim. (If you as rescuer have any misgivings about this piece, don't try ascending to the victim.) Here is a condensed overview of the procedure.

Step 1: Rearrange and reinforce your anchor to securely hold an upward force. (If you are on the first pitch, you may need to build an anchor with several upward-force components.) Escape the belay.

Step 2: Ascend to the victim. Since the rope strand will be anchored taut, preventing you from tying figure-eight backups, you will use a third friction hitch as your backup as you make upward progress. **(Note: This ascent is hazardous, with potentially dire consequences should the leader's top piece fail.)**

Step 3: Reinforce the piece holding you and the leader to form a solid anchor. Attach the victim to this anchor with a load-releasing knot.

Step 4: Attach yourself to the anchor and descend back to the original anchor using appropriate backups, and disassemble it.

Step 5: Re-ascend to victim, cleaning the pitch as you go.

Step 6: Lower the victim or perform an assisted rappel.

Because of the complexity and potential hazards of leader rescue, it's an advanced self-rescue skill. I cover it briefly only to give you a general understanding of how it utilizes techniques described earlier in this chapter. May the description inspire you to learn this skill when you're ready from an experienced mentor or professional.

Chapter 8

Knot Craft and Gear Tricks

KNOTS & HITCHES

Understanding the application of knots is as important as knowing how to tie them. Though basic guidelines exist, in many situations you have choices. What is the best knot for the task at hand? As with other climbing decisions, weigh the pros and cons before making your choice.

By paying close attention to your task and avoiding distractions, you can ensure the integrity of every knot you tie. Cinch each knot down tightly, tying it neatly so your partner can evaluate it easily from a distance. Whenever applicable, leave a minimum of a 4" (10.2cm) tail. Tighten newly-tied permanent knots with extra gusto and monitor them closely. Use extra care with new ropes and webbing, which are slick and prone to slippage.

Basic knots commonly used by trad climbers include the following:

Figure-eight Follow-Through (aka Rewoven Figure-eight) *(Photos: 1-5, below)*

Due to its high level of strength and difficulty in untying, the *figure-eight follow-through* makes an ideal tie-in knot (and is the *only* tie-in knot I recommend for trad climbing). Allow approximately 8" (25.5cm) to finish it with half of a double fisherman's knot.

Figure-eight On a Bight (Photos: 1-3, below)

The strongest knot for clipping into the anchor is the figure-eight on a bight. Its drawbacks in this application include a lack of adjustability, and its requiring a significantly large amount of rope to tie. This knot can also be used to clip into the rope with a locking carabiner when you're leading in blocks (see Chapter 6).

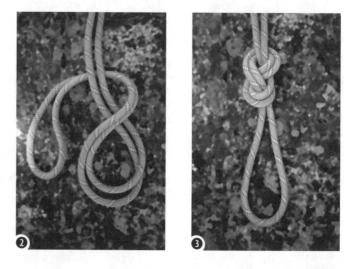

Clove Hitch (Photos: 1 and 2, below)

The clove hitch can also be used to clip into anchors. What it lacks in security as a hitch, and strength (about 10 percent weaker than the figure-eight), it sometimes makes up for in static clip-ins because of its adjustability. When rope availability is an issue, it is also desirable as it requires very little. For it to be effective, though, you

To load

must tighten each strand after creating the hitch, with the load strand in line with the carabiner spine. Otherwise its strength is compromised by up to 30 percent.

Overhand On a Bight *(Photo: right)*

Although it provides slightly less strength than the figure-eight on a bight, the *overhand on a bight* is another secure knot for tying into an anchor. It requires less rope than the figure-eight but more than the clove hitch. Once weighted, however, it is more difficult to untie than the figure-eight on a bight.

Girth Hitch *(Photos: 1-3, below)*

Though appropriate for many tasks, the girth hitch is most commonly used to clip a cow's tail or a daisy chain into your harness. Use it also to join two slings together.

Overhand on a Bight

Double Fisherman's (aka Grapevine)

(Photos: 1-6, below)

The double fisherman's is one of the most common knots used to tie two ropes together for rappelling. Because of its bulky profile, use it on rappels where terrain is steep or overhanging. Because it is difficult to untie once weighted, it is also a good choice for tying permanent knots in cord and webbing (e.g. making runners and tying cordelettes). For tying together two, different-diameter ropes or for extra security, add another wrap on each side to make a triple fisherman's.

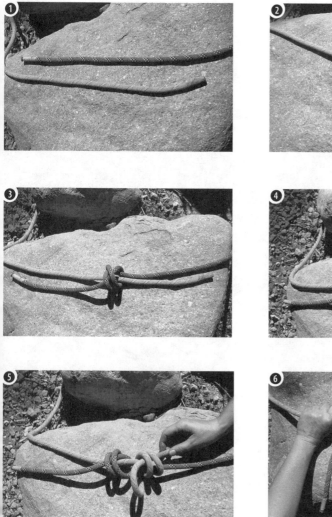
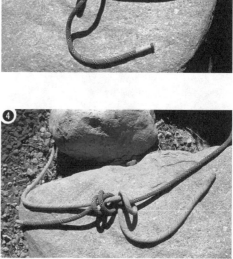

Flat Overhand *(Photos: 1 and 2, right)*

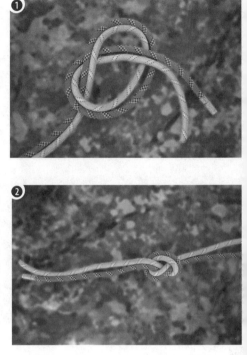

The flat overhand is appropriate for joining ropes of similar diameter that are likely to receive low-load forces (as in rappelling). Although not as strong as the double fisherman's this knot runs far more smoothly over rope-snagging terrain. Because of this feature it has been popular in Europe for years, and is finally catching on in the US, where it was once unknowingly called the "death knot," seeming too simple for such a responsibility! For those still doubtful of the flat overhand's performance for connecting rappel ropes, tests conducted in the late '90s found it safe and effective for tying similar-diameter rope and cord ends together, provided you allow an adequate tail on each end of the knot—enough to allow it to invert one time. The flat overhand is, however, difficult to untie once weighted.

Ring Bend (aka Water or Tape knot)

(Photos: 1-4 next page)

The ring bend is a good choice when tying together webbing that is 1" (10cm) diameter or larger. Although particularly good for a permanent knot, the ring bend can be more easily loosened than the fisherman's knots when freshly tied, so monitor it carefully until the force of several loads has tightened it. One bonus is that the ring bend requires less material to tie than the double or triple fisherman's. Also, because of its bulky profile it wedges nicely into constricting cracks—if needed in a pinch for protection.

Ring Bend (aka Water or Tape knot)

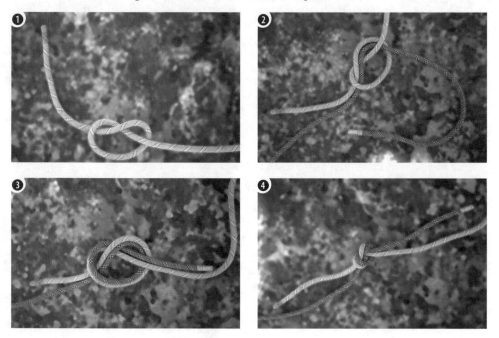

Double Bowline

The double bowline is sometimes the preferred tie-in knot for sport climbers because it unties easier than the figure-eight follow through. But, because it is so easily untied, it has resulted in several injuries and deaths. For this reason it is neither recommended nor illustrated in this text. It is, however, useful for anchoring the ends of ropes around trees or other natural features. Refer to Luebben's *Knots for Climbers*, listed in Resources for a description.

IMPROVISATION TECHNIQUES

Trad adventures hold many surprises, requiring adaptability on the part of climbers. Although the "keep it simple" adage often applies, enhancing your repertoire of tools and methods increases your ability to handle tricky scenarios. You'll have to improvise in situations where conventional gear and solutions are unavailable, but at other times it's just comforting to have a choice.

Prepare yourself to think on your toes with these simple alternatives that can come into play on lead, at the belay, or on rappel.

Carabiner Brake Rappel

The carabiner brake can provide a smooth rappel ride for climbers who have either forgotten or dropped their rappel device. While ovals are best suited for this configuration, standard Ds also work.

(Photos: 1-4, below) Attach two carabiners with the gates reversed and opposed (see Chapter 4) to a locking 'biner that you clipped to your harness belay/rappel loop. Next, feed two equal bights of the rappel line into these two carabiners so that the line leading to the anchor is at the top, and the line leading to the ground is at the bottom. Now take two additional 'biners and clip them perpendicular to the first two underneath the rope bights, gates reversed and facing down (away from you). This is crucial: carabiners with gates facing up can unclip from the weight of the rope. If you want more friction (for a steeper rappel or when using a smaller diameter rope), add another 'biner.

Rope goes to anchor

Brakeline

Climber: Dave Nettle

Years Trad Free Climbing: 30

Average Trad Lead Ability: 5.11

Favorite Trad Climbing Area:
   Sierra backcountry

Most Respected Trad Free
   Climber: Peter Croft

Dave Nettle Collection

Advanced Techniques for Backcountry Efficiency

Efficiency is the most valuable skill you can learn as a trad climbing newcomer, especially on long rock routes in the backcountry. Efficiency is often translated as climbing fast and placing gear quickly. But these are skills that time will usually teach. For now, follow experienced leaders on backcountry routes and observe how belays are set up and rope is managed.

If you pay close attention to your backcountry mentors, you might also be fortunate enough to pick up a handful of key trad "tricks" that also support efficiency, namely *simul-climbing, back-cleaning,* and *walking pro*. These are advanced and often risky techniques, but nonetheless essential if you have your sights set on climbing difficult backcountry routes fast and efficiently with a lean rack.

Walking Pro

When climbing a crack of the same size for a long distance, a light rack might dictate that you choose between a long runout or "walking" a single piece upward every few moves. Always try to situate yourself in the most solid stance possible before sliding the piece up. The obvious danger is that you place increasing distance between you and your last stationary piece, and if you fall while sliding your piece up, you could take a real screamer. Keep your eyes peeled for protection possibilities in surrounding features—be sure to sling these.

Back-Cleaning

Not as risky is back-cleaning a similar section with two pieces. Set the first one, climb slightly past it (but not so far that you can't reach

Continued on next page

it) then set your second piece. Once the rope is clipped, reach down and remove and unclip the first piece, move up and repeat. This technique is known as *leap-frogging* and employs the art of back-cleaning. Back-cleaning is also helpful on a long pitch when you need to conserve gear, or on a route that you know requires the exact piece of protection you placed previously on a difficult section higher up.

It pays to look ahead on pitches to see which pieces may be needed again. There is no need to back-clean if a piece won't be needed higher. Generally when I find an opportunity for a bomber Stopper placement, I'll set it and leave it for pro, back-cleaning more versatile cams for later. Back-cleaning is also a great way to reduce rope drag which is exactly that—a drag! If you ever get to a point where you must lower off a piece to back-clean several lower placements, lower to the *last* (furthest) piece first and clean on the way up. This keeps multiple pieces protecting your "top-rope" while fiddling around.

Simul-Climbing

Finally, simul-climbing is handy on terrain that is relatively easy for both leader and follower, and allows rapid coverage of long stretches of your route. Begin with the usual belay-leader roles, and when the rope comes tight, the sec-ond begins climbing simultaneously, cleaning pieces along the way. Try your best to climb at a similar pace, and always keep at least three pieces of solid gear between partners. If your rope is longer than 165' (50m) or this practice is new to you, use more. Try not to let slack rope pile up between you, and be careful not to pull your partner off the rock by unnecessary rope tension. Note that you need to take every precaution to *not* fall, so don't attempt this on difficult terrain, or when conditions prevent partners from communicating with one another. Simul-climbing inadvertently may be necessary when a leader is combining two pitches and needs more rope to reach a belay, or has accidentally passed a belay ledge and needs a few extra feet to reach a stance with adequate anchor options.

On easier ground when a team knows it will be simul-climbing for a distance it's best for the second to shoulder coil half the rope then clip into the middle (with a locking carabiner). This eliminates rope drag, makes it easier to manage slack, and helps communication. A good trick is for the second to leave the rope in their belay device so that if the leader calls for a belay, the follower simply places a few pieces of gear, clips in, and resumes a safe and timely belay.

—Dave Nettle

Munter Hitch

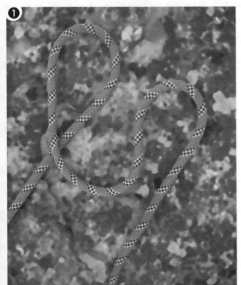

Munter Belay

The Munter hitch *(Photos: 1 and 2, left)* has numerous applications including use as a belay mechanism. Because the longest leader fall I ever held was a 50-foot (16.6m) screamer that was halted by this simple hitch, I'm a big fan of the Munter belay. Use it on your harness to belay leaders or followers; or directly off the anchor to belay followers.

When you belay with a Munter, the hitch will shift (or "pop") from one side of the carabiner to the other, depending on whether you're feeding rope out or taking it in. To lock it, bring your brake line parallel with the strand leading to the climber.

A *Munter belay* directly off the anchor *(Photo: opposite page, top)* is ideal for belaying the second when you are absolutely positive your anchor is bomber. Not only does this system provide a built-in directional to keep the weight off your waist when your partner falls, it eliminates the need to escape the belay during self-rescue. Because of this, it is the preferred belay method for professional guides with seconding clients. Belaying with a Munter directly off the anchor is not appropriate when belaying a leader. Climbers new to gear placement should consider getting a few years experience building anchors before using this method. (Note: Do not use friction belay devices to belay in this manner.)

Hip Belay *(Illustration: below right)*

Using the body as friction for belaying was standard practice for decades before the introduction of today's belay devices. Virtually outmoded by modern technology, the hip belay remains practical when you do not have time to prepare a standard belay, or lack gear. Keep in mind that it can be extremely dangerous; it's never recommended for belaying a leader.

Face the climber requiring the belay and take in any slack as you would before any other belay. Now wrap the rope around the backside of your lower torso, hands positioned alongside each hip. The hand grasping the strand leading directly to the slack line is your brake hand. As your partner climbs, use the same rope-handling technique you use with your device to take in slack, without letting go with your brake hand. If a fall occurs, wrap the rope across your pelvis with your brake hand, creating as much friction as possible. Be careful how you position yourself between the climber and your anchor; if positioned improperly, the weight of the climber could cause the rope to "unwind." If this occurs, you will lose control of the rope and probably drop your partner. Use this belay method only on low-angle terrain with a solid stance or anchor, when you don't have the time or gear to belay with a device.

Munter belay off the masterpoint

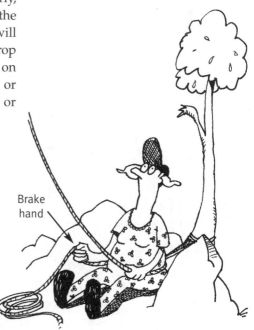

Bowline On a Coil

(Illustrations: 1 and 2 left, 3-6 opposite page)

Picture this: You're hiking to the base of a climb and the approach or descent has become technical and exposed. You're wishing you had a belay, but your harness is tucked away in the bottom of the pack. Forget the harness, tie directly into the rope with a *bowline on a coil*, and ask your partner to belay you from above.

Wrap the end of the rope around your waist four times, leaving about an arm's length of slack as a tail. Now take a bight of the line leading to the belayer and bring it up and under the coils at belly-button level. Give it a twist so that the line closest to your body leads down and out to the remainder of the rope. Now bend the loop down and over the four wrapped coils and push a small bight of the rope leading to the belayer up from underneath into the loop. Finally, take the short rope tail and slide it through this bight. Tighten by tugging firmly on the rope leading to the belayer. Use half a double fisherman's knot to tie the tail off around the coils. Climb on.

The bowline on a coil should only be used when you have no other immediate options, and should be avoided by anyone leading. Before using this tie-in alternative, consider that a fall with enough force could break your ribs.

3 turns around body

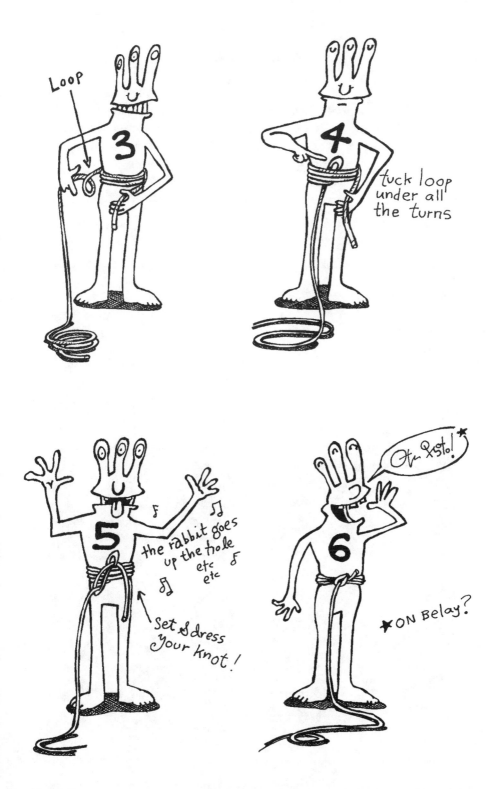

Rope-Equalized Anchoring

If you don't have your cordelette or Web-o-lette™, it's possible to create an equalized anchor system using only the rope. Although the following method requires a lot of rope and is harder to escape in a self-rescue scenario, it provides a valuable anchoring option without sacrificing equalization. Before using this method, be sure your next pitch isn't a rope stretcher, requiring every available inch. *(Photos: sidebar below and right)*

Double Figure Eight Equalization

Tie a figure eight on a bight with an extra-large loop of rope. Now feed the loop through the strands forming the top of the figure eight to create three loops to equalize each of your three anchor components. (Use the three loops you created to clip into your pieces.)

Continued on next page

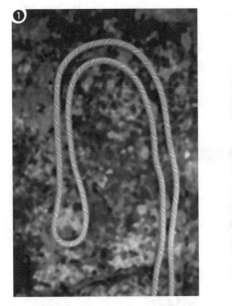

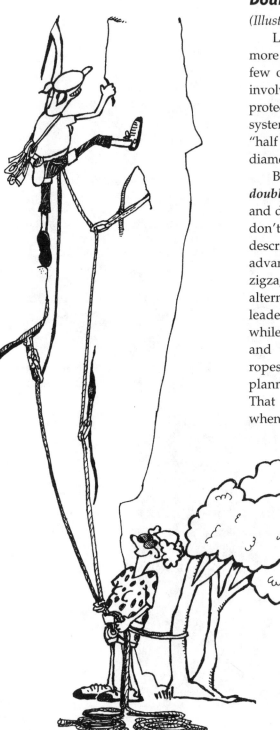

Double-Rope Lead Technique

(Illustration: left)

Leading with two ropes, which is more common in Great Britain and a few other countries than in the US, involves clipping alternate ropes into protection. The ropes used for this system are (confusingly) known as "half ropes," but are only smaller in diameter than standard single ropes.

Best reserved for expert leaders, *double-rope leading* has both benefits and drawbacks (with many do's and don'ts, most of which are not described in this overview). It's most advantageous on an indirect route zigzagging its way up the rock. By alternately clipping each line, the leader experiences less rope drag while reducing reliance on runners and slings. Always carrying two ropes also benefits you during planned and unplanned descents. That extra rope can save the day when one gets stuck or damaged.

The major system drawback relates to your alternately clipping each line into lead protection—at any one time you are solely trusting a single half rope. (Though you could clip both ropes, there are times when this is inadvisable.) Because carrying two lines increases the chance of confusion and rope tangles, it requires advanced rope-management skills for both leader and belayer. Belaying with half ropes takes practice, and requires only certain tubes and plates (figure-eight devices are not an option). A belayer must master feeding out and taking in one rope at a time, while consistently monitoring appropriate tension or slack in each line.

Half ropes are advertised as such by manufacturers, and should be purchased as a pair. Using two, unlike diameter ropes results in uneven wear and is dangerous.

Chapter 9

Common Know-How

RATINGS

Class Ratings

There are several free climbing rating systems in use today. Americans and Canadians rely on the *Yosemite Decimal System*, an elaboration of *Class Ratings*, which was developed by the Sierra Club in the 1930s. In Class Ratings a class is assigned to terrain depending on its physical and technical difficulty. Because assessing difficulty tends to be fairly subjective, I've added risk factors and the consequences of an unroped fall to differentiate Classes 1-5.

Classes 1-6

Class 1—Hiking. Minimal risk.

Class 2—Simple scrambling on minimally exposed boulders and rocks, with the occasional need to use your hands for balance. Low risk.

Class 3—Moderate scrambling (with hands and feet) on rock in an often exposed environment. A rope should be considered for beginner climbers. An unroped fall could be fatal or result in serious injuries.

Class 4—Technical and exposed scrambling in which a rope should be considered, particularly for beginners. An unroped fall far from the ground would most likely be fatal.

Class 5—Technical climbing requiring a rope, belay, and equipment. An unroped fall far from the ground would be fatal.

Class 6—Direct-Aid Climbing.

Yosemite Decimal System

The Yosemite Decimal System (YDS) extends from the Class 5 rating, numbering from 5.1 to 5.14, with a & b (or "-") and c & d (or "+") increments 5.10 and above. Objectively and in theory, the lower the number, the easier the route. But since in reality ratings are highly subjective, depending on physical differences (height, etc.) and terrain familiarity, each route will feel a little different to each climber. Because of this, ratings cannot be the final authority on route difficulty. Use them in combination with other analysis and research in determining which routes you're capable of climbing.

Guidebook authors aren't responsible for rating climbs; they simply collect and compile data from local resources. Routes are most often rated initially by first ascent parties. Many parties encourage feedback from subsequent teams to develop a rating by group consensus. Although rare, some routes are later either down-rated or up-rated based on collective agreement, usually among local climbers. This is likely particularly if a key hold breaks, altering the climb's anatomy and therefore its difficulty level.

YDS ratings traditionally reflect the single most difficult move on a route or pitch. That means that a pitch with several 5.11 moves receives a 5.11 rating, while the same rating is given to a route with 165' of continuous 5.7 with only one 5.11 move. Obviously climbing continuous 5.11 requires a stronger, more skilled climber than accomplishing one move of 5.11. Nevertheless, the ratings are the same. Yet, depending on the area, climbers may factor in other considerations when rating climbs. If a pitch is strenuous, sustained, or very exposed, it might receive one rating higher than the most difficult move.

Protection Severity Ratings

An additional rating system of G, PG, R, and X, which is becoming more common today, indicates that protection is good, pretty good, seriously runout, or extremely runout with severe consequences, respectively. This system alerts climbers to protection issues that help them choose the appropriate climb not just for their physical abilities but also for their technical skill levels.

Grades

Multipitch rock routes are assigned a YDS rating (based on the most difficult pitch), as well as a *grade*. Grades were first used in the 1950s in Yosemite, and later codified under the National Climbing Classification System (NCCS). This system generally describes the length of a route, the time needed to ascend it, and the general technical difficulty—for an average experienced climber (assuming competence for the expected level of climbing).

Grades I-VI

I—A few pitches, requiring approximately 1-3 hours.

II—Several pitches, requiring a half day.

III—Several pitches, requiring a full day.

IV—Several pitches of moderate climbing difficulty, requiring a full day.

V—Multiple pitches of moderate to advanced climbing, requiring one to two days. Can involve a bivouac, but may be done by experts in a day.

VI—Multiple pitches requiring two or more days, involving difficult climbing.

The grade system, which is clearly very subjective, can only serve as a general benchmark. Today talented and fast free climbers are challenging this system. For instance, The Nose on El Capitan, probably the world's most famous Grade VI, was first climbed in a total of 47 (non-consecutive) days in 1957. Two years later, its first continuous ascent was completed in six days. Many climbers now complete The Nose in under 24 hours. Recently, a team climbed *two* Grade VI routes—the northwest face of Half Dome *and* The Nose—in a day.

While these extremely talented athletes are no doubt exceptional, NCCS grade classifications are becoming less meaningful in light of such endeavors.

Rating Translation & Style

When exploring a new style of climbing, people commonly assume that their capabilities in one style will transfer directly over. This happens frequently when sport climbers are breaking into traditional climbing, or when front-country trad climbers get on backcountry terrain. In the sport realm a 5.9 rating is generally considered "easy." Some sport enthusiasts may have climbed a 5.9 on their first day at the crags and never again; their idea of "hard" is most likely 5.11 and above. Yet, for new trad climbers 5.9 is usually difficult. So difficult, in fact, that even a 5.11-capable sport-climbing specialist may experience a significant struggle on a 5.9 crack.

More often than not, rating differences are due to your concentration on a particular climbing style. If you have basic crack technique wired, a 5.9 crack isn't going to challenge you as much as if you had focused largely on mastering the delicate and balanced moves required on steep, bolted faces. Because the mental and physical demands of sport climbing and trad climbing are quite different, those that enjoy both styles often take days, and sometimes weeks or months, to get muscles and mind into sync with each style.

Relying on ratings as your sole barometer of progress is a huge pitfall. There are many ways to improve that have little to do with the numbers game. For years I couldn't lead anything rated higher than 5.10a/b—a common plateau for many trad leaders. So I focused on doing as many climbs as I could within the 5.8-5.9 range, and doing them well. I had a lot of fun once I let go of my attachment to high numbers. After several years I noticed a huge improvement in my overall intuition and comfort on the rock. I built anchors with proficiency and speed, and improved my rope-management skills tenfold. As a result, I became more comfortable *on-sighting* routes, ascending various rock types in new and different areas, climbing in the backcountry, and doing longer routes. When I felt capable of attempting climbs with higher ratings, my core experience had expanded such that I had a better chance of succeeding, and of succeeding safely. When you recognize that improvement often comes in small but significant increments, you'll no longer be a slave to ratings.

CLIMBING ETIQUETTE

The "my beach—my wave" philosophy in climbing is rarely tolerated. Most climbers welcome the opportunity to share their local crags with others, and in the process meet new people from different areas. Nevertheless, awkward moments occur when someone's personal space is encroached upon, or a climber's "right" to climb is squelched. Although few hard-and-fast rules exist, if climbers are aware of regional guidelines and act with respect and courtesy, any issue can be resolved in a civil manner.

Common Cragging Courtesy

You'll easily resolve, if not completely avoid, possible conflicts at US crags by adhering to these basic guidelines of climbing etiquette:

• Though some negotiations may occur, generally climbers who reach the base of a route before you have dibs on starting first. A team that gets up early and packs its gear the night beforehand usually is the first party at the base—and they've earned the right to start the route.

• If you find yourself behind a slow team on a long route and are considering passing them, obtain their consent first, and then pass at an appropriate location like a belay with a large stance. Be absolutely certain your team will move quickly enough to stay ahead of them. If they refuse to allow a pass, accept their prerogative. Get up earlier next time.

• On crowded multipitch routes, wait for the follower of the team ahead to reach the next belay stance before you start leading that same pitch. This courtesy prevents crowding at small belay ledges.

• When top-roping several climbs side by side at popular locales, consider that other climbers may wish to lead those climbs. Avoid tying up many routes at one time and, when your group has finished, remove your ropes as soon as possible. If one of the climbs you've set up isn't in use and other climbers indicate a desire to lead it, move your rope aside to allow passage.

• Never clip into any protection or anchors already in use without permission.

• Don't throw your rope near someone who is climbing without ample warning, especially if he or she is leading.

Leave No Trace

Future use of many climbing areas depends largely on how well we practice minimum-impact principles. Though climbers are generally an environmentally conscious group, we can be careless, lazy, and sometimes uninformed. Besides being a great ethical concept, Leave No Trace (LNT) is a national program devoted to educating outdoor enthusiasts on these principles. Begun as a government program, LNT was run for awhile by the National Outdoor Leadership School (NOLS), and is now is an independent non-profit organization based in Boulder, Colorado. LNT hopes to change behavior through education, basing their guidelines on "abiding respect for and appreciation of wild and unique places and their inhabitants." Many suggestions in this section derive from LNT guidelines.

Inappropriate disposal of human waste, litter, and erosion are the three major ways climbers impact the environment. Cutting established trails in haste creates erosion. In populated regions, follow the most obvious trail up to the base of crags as well as when descending. When traversing where no trails exist, spread your party out on stable ground to avoid creating new paths. Avoid fragile areas like meadows, steep hillsides, and the delicate black cryptogam you encounter in desert regions. Respect flora at the base of routes by not removing or trimming bushes or plants.

Camp in existing sites (if possible) at least 200' from water. Resist temptation to "improve" a campsite by moving natural features, and don't dig drainage ditches around your tent. Build fires, where allowed, only in established fire rings. Burn wood from home, or collect small dead pieces from the ground well away from trails and camp to diffuse your impact. Don't make fires in fragile alpine regions, or directly at rock bases, where they leave scars lasting decades. If you're going to sleep at the base of a route, don't build a fire.

An unplanned bivy in cold nighttime temperatures may dictate a fire for comfort or survival. In this case, build a fire ring in dirt or sand, away from dry leaves or timber. Dispose of ash when cold by dispersing it widely. Deconstruct the ring and return the site to its original state.

Energy bar wrappers, climbing tape, spilled chalk, cigarette butts, toilet paper, and feces are all evidence of careless climbers. Although most climbers pack out bulky food wrappers, they're often careless with wrapper corners and gel packets torn off and tossed (with great intention) into packs and pockets. Yet, when a jacket or topo is hastily retrieved, trash can fall out as well. I keep a small Ziploc™ on hand to contain my trash within my pack.

And then there are land mines—piles of feces coiled carelessly behind a bush or a crag, when the pressure of leading hits us in the gut and we gotta go. Bury human feces at least 6" (15cm) below ground 200' (60m) from trails, campsites, water sources, and drainage areas. Because this may not be possible in alpine environments, find a sunny location and smear feces in thin layers on a rock. However gross and unsanitary, it dries quickly and disintegrates. For sanitizing your hands afterward carry antibacterial handy-wipes, which reduce the risk of passing fecal-borne bacteria to your partner. Pack your toilet paper out, or, better yet, use natural objects for wiping such as rocks, leaves, or sticks.

Should you need to urinate mid-climb, avoid the wall and pee off into space—in a direction other than the likely approach of climbers from below! Recently a friend returned from climbing the crowded Nose route on El Capitan and reported being urinated upon by a climber on a ledge above, waiting his turn for the next pitch. As she was leading, she felt a few droplets of moisture, which she thought oddly was rain—it was a stellar bluebird day. When she glanced up and realized it was urine, she was horrified. Hearing her story temporarily curbed my interest in that climb. If on a ledge, always urinate (or defecate) as far from the most obvious belay location as possible. In remote areas, find a flat rock, deposit your feces upon it, and toss it off the route. Never do this if there is the slightest chance you could clobber a climber or hiker below.

Access

Though access to climbing areas is always threatened, thanks to a few non-profit climbing organizations, climbers have the representation of a group of dedicated individuals working throughout the US for continued access. These groups help reduce climber impact by organizing crag-cleanup days, cosponsoring outhouse installation in high-use areas, and organizing trail-building efforts. They also employ active lobbyists and lawyers to fight legal-access encroachments.

Most access issues involve conflicts with private or public land managers and owners, and are often related to perceived climber impact. Although pro-access organizations generally have the environment's best interests in mind, their often hard-line uncompromising approach has driven a wedge between some environmental groups and the climbing community. In fact, some conservationists have begun viewing climbing as just another extractive recreation industry, lumping climbers in the same category as, say, snowmobile users. The voice of climbers has sometimes been heard as shouting, *We want to climb where we want, when we want, and how we want*. This is a distressing image, especially for climbers with steadfast conservation principles.

Through negotiations and compromises with environmental groups, we all benefit more than through hard-line opposition. If you're a climber who supports access but also wants environmental values to be fairly represented, join various access organizations and let your voice be heard. Follow the issues and stay informed by getting the facts from both sides. Avoid knee-jerk reactions and take thoughtful stances based on your own principles. When you become aware of issues affecting the backcountry, climbing, or your favorite climbing areas, write your Representative and Senators; urge your friends and climbing partners to do the same. In addition, support legislative moves to obtain more national recreation land and preserve existing areas.

Chapter 10

Conclusion

Congratulations. Your journey into traditional lead climbing is well underway with this book's concepts fresh in your mind. You've set the foundation that can provide you with a lifetime of profoundly satisfying challenges. Stick around; you won't regret it.

Every effort you make has one primary purpose: the refinement of your skills through pure repetition. The nature of trad climbing does not allow you to think your way toward excellence; proficiency grows through logging in hundreds of hours on the rocks. Outside the sphere of trad climbing, one might consider the concept of "stimulating repetition" an oxymoron. Not so on the sharp end of the gear-leader. I guarantee no two experiences will ever be the same. It's simply not possible.

Since picking up this book, you've examined the specific equipment, skills, and techniques that make trad leading a unique experience, rich in adventure, and vastly different from other free climbing styles. An overview of specific tools was provided to give you enough facts to make informed choices when you purchase the arsenal of gear you'll need to safely cope with the technical demands on trad terrain. You may be broke after your initial spree, but the experiences ahead come at no cost. No one's collecting entrance fees at the base of El Cap (yet!) and aside from paying an occasional wilderness permit or park fee, climbing on most of the world's rock faces is available to us for free. All you have to do is show up.

I hope you have begun your new relationship with trad leading in low-risk settings that allow for a wide margin of error. If you familiarize yourself on the ground with the unique capabilities of your gear by creating anchor systems under the watchful eye of a seasoned guide, you'll enjoy a huge pay off once you're on your own and climbing with partners who have entrusted you with their lives. When your gear placement and anchors get thumbs up from your mentor, the safety net of a top-rope will let you to further orchestrate these new skills with movement and additional technical tasks without the worry of a fatal error. Work out the kinks on top-rope; when you're ready to shed your training wheels, you'll benefit not only from your technical know-how. . . you will also be more confident than if you had plunged right in without a safety net.

When you're ready to venture onto easy trad ground sans a top-rope, you'll be primed for learning more technical tasks that are essential to safe and enjoyable leading. Then the stakes are higher: the keys to survival are a smart route and good partner choices, as well as developing careful attention to detail. If you push your limits safely and sanely, what follows is improved ability and technical prowess that allows access to the crown jewel of traditional leading: the multipitch adventure. At that point, even more techniques will be introduced, and once again, you will need that all important careful attention to detail. By now your anchoring and protection placement skills have become intuitive, and you're not struggling as much with the climbing itself. But the stakes are raised yet another notch forcing you to consider that the higher you climb, the more responsibility you have. Back-up plans are a must, as are basic self-rescue skills. As climbers, we must recognize that the freedom we sometimes take for granted in the sport stems largely from an understood agreement that we are also taking full responsibility for our adventures. We don't rely on outside rescue services to save our butts, and we don't sue land managers for mishaps.

Eventually you'll find yourself leading trad routes several pitches from the ground in magnificent settings marveling over your good fortune to have finally achieved the expertise that got you this far. Your elation can fuel plans for bigger, harder, faster ascents. You're in luck if you haven't tossed your Beginner's Mind to the wind. There's still plenty to learn, from etiquette to improvisation techniques, as well as more advanced skills not covered in this book. Look for every possible chance to continuing learning from more skilled climbers, and keep in mind there's rarely only one way to accomplish any technical task. This book provides what I consider the bare bones knowledge for trad adventures; there's a lot more information out there for you to learn.

From this point forward, your positive and humble attitude will keep bring you great partners, learning opportunities, and overall safety and enjoyment. Humility is really the key—arrogance places a tremendous burden on any climber, especially the new leader. When your attitude reeks of superiority, you're engaging in a losing battle that demands you to live up to a standard of unobtainable perfection—especially for a new leader. If you're confident, that's great. Let that confidence slip into arrogance, and people expect far more from you than you can deliver as a beginner. Strive for excellence with your ego in check, and learn to accept foibles as positive growth opportunities. Every person and every experience teaches us something of value, something new.

Finally, don't give up your other climbing interests in pursuit of the ultimate trad experience. The real beauty of trad climbing is its incorporation of all other styles of climbing. Variety is not only enjoyable but it prevents burnout and is beneficial to your technique. The best trad climbers I know divide their time away from trad stone between bouldering, hard top-roping, sport cragging, aid climbing, and even ice climbing in the winter. And with more experience under your belt, don't miss out on the opportunities to venture away from your home crags to climb on different rock at varied areas. Visiting new areas keeps your experience fresh and hones your ability to adapt to different rock, ratings, and conditions. As they say, it's all good.

Climb on. . .

Appendix 1:

The Clean Climbing Revolution

The Clean Climbing Revolution accomplished two major events in rock-climbing history. It raised consciousness among free climbers about the nonrenewable resource of rock, and provided a solution that inadvertently led to some of the most important technological advances within the sport. The evolution of hammerless protection in the US took off in 1967 when Royal Robbins returned from a climbing trip to Britain where he'd observed climbers using pebbles as removable lead protection. Back in Yosemite, Robbins and his wife Liz completed the famed Nutcracker, quite possibly the first, clean first ascent in the country. Shortly thereafter, Robbins wrote a short piece on his experience for *Summit*, which inspired his peers to pursue clean climbing.

Climbers began experimenting with the use of common machine nuts for protection, and soon it became possible to order limited removable protection from overseas. In 1971, Doug Robinson completed the first clean Grade IV in Yosemite Valley (East Buttress of Middle Cathedral) with partner Jay Jensen. During this time Robinson and fellow climbers Tom Frost and Yvon Chouinard began tinkering with design ideas for additional removable-protection options, eventually leading to the production of Chouinard's Hexcentrics and Stoppers. In 1972 these items were offered in the first official Chouinard Equipment Company (since sold and renamed Black Diamond) catalog, along with Robinson's essay "The Whole Natural Art of Climbing Protection," one of the most noted, quoted, reprinted, and influential pieces of climbing literature to date.

Within months of the article's publication, everyone seemed to be climbing clean," says Robinson. The first paragraph captures the essence of his message:

There is a word for it, and that word is clean. Climbing with only nuts and runners for protection is clean climbing. Clean because the rock is left unaltered by the passing climber. Clean because nothing is hammered into the rock and then hammered back out, leaving the rock scarred and the next climber's experience less natural. Clean because the climber's protection leaves little trace of his ascension. Clean is climbing the rock without changing it, a step closer to organic climbing for the natural man.

Robinson eventually created the tube chock, a large cylindrical device for protecting off-widths. The Lowe Tri-Cam was developed and commercially distributed in the mid-'70s, followed by Yosemite climber Ray Jardine's revolutionary invention in 1978 of the "Friend," the first spring-loaded camming device (SLCD). By the late '70s, these new options, all relatively lightweight and easy to place, virtually eliminated the average climber's need or desire to use pitons, especially on free routes.

Appendix 2:

Lead Ascent Styles

Numerous lead-ascent styles exist today, each requiring a certain level of technical assistance. Used in both trad free climbing and sport climbing, these styles include:

- **On-Sight Flash:** This most impressive and bold lead involves a first-time, no-falls ascent by a climber who has neither received any details (beta) regarding the route nor watched another climber ascend it. This ascent style also requires the leader place all his or her protection on lead (rather than pre-placing it on rappel).

- **Flash:** This ascent denotes leading a route for the first time, placing all protection on lead, and succeeding with no falls or hangs. On a flash ascent, though, the leader may have received previous beta or viewed another leader on the route.

- **Red-point:** In this ascent the climber works a route by taking frequent tension from the belayer, hanging on the rope and resting between difficult sections. Once each section is mastered, the climber attempts to lead it from ground to top in one push without falling or hanging. A climber might achieve a red-point after working a route in an afternoon, or years later.

- **Pink Point:** Otherwise similar to the red-point, this ascent style allows the pre-placement of lead protection on rappel.

- **Head Point:** A style that originated in Britain and common on bold, runout routes, a head-point ascent is when the leader rehearses the route on top-rope, and leads the route when ready, placing sparse protection from the ground up, hopefully summiting without a fall.

Appendix 3:

Developments Before Sport Climbing

Almost a decade before the advent of sport climbing, worldwide free-climbing styles, particularly in Europe, suggested a change was coming. French climbers were establishing bolted routes via rappel in the Verdon Gorge in the late 1970s and very early 1980s. Their lack of hesitance to use protection to gain upward purchase on free climbs spawned the term "French-free." Around the same time, climbers Tony Yaniro and Ray Jardine were incorporating rehearsal methods, pre-placed gear, and *hang-dogging* (resting on gear between difficult moves) into their tactics to establish America's first 5.13s. In Germany, climbers were using similar rehearsal methods for no-fall/hang attempts on the extremely difficult walls of the Frankenjura. Ironically, it was here that the term "red-point" came into use: once a climb had been led in the Frankenjura without falls or hangs, a red dot was painted at the base of each route.

Appendix 4:

The Fixed-Line & Drilled-Bolt Controversy

Between the late '50s and early '70s, first-ascent tactics on some of the most renowned Yosemite walls came under fire by a faction of climbers. The controversy focused on two issues: a team's reliance upon fixed lines and excessive use of drilled bolts. Fixed ropes allowed teams to linger on routes for months—even years—letting team members periodically retreat to the Valley floor for supplies, rest, and food. Different partners often rotated in and out of each team, and entire seasons sometimes passed with little or no route progress. What came to be known as siege climbing was then termed by climber Warren Harding an "expedition-style mentality."

The seemingly high number of bolts placed on some first ascents was also criticized. Bolts provided instant protection and aid points on blank walls, allowing passage up sections that some believed should have been left blank and either unclimbed or climbed by some other means. Most controversial of such ascents was Harding's route up the West Face of the Leaning Tower in 1961, and his establishment of the Dawn Wall (aka The Wall of Early Morning Light) on El Capitan in 1970. Harding's Leaning Tower ascent involved 111 bolts placed on the 800' wall during 18 days over five months; the Dawn Wall had over 300 holes drilled (some for bolts, others for hooks) during 27 continuous days on 2800' of rock. Although Harding and his partner Dean Caldwell didn't use siege tactics on the Dawn Wall, they did place an enormous number of bolts.

Among others offended by Harding's techniques during this period was Royal Robbins. The following passage from Pat Ament's *Spirit of the Age*, a 1992 biography of Robbins, best illustrates his view of such tactics: "Given enough bolts and time, any rock of any size and difficulty could be climbed." Robbins thought that to have the certitude of bolts, and to string fixed ropes from the bottom of the wall to its top, diminished the adventure.

Though Robbins initially denounced Harding's infamous siege and bolting tactics, it later seemed that he had something of a change of heart. On the first ascent of the Salathé Wall on El Capitan in 1961, his team used fixed lines on the lower third of the route (a trend still popular today). Nine years later he set out to remove bolts placed on what he called the "contrived and artificial" Dawn Wall route, on its second ascent. Finding the climb far more technically challenging than he'd anticipated, he and his partner Don Lauria stopped chopping after the first four pitches. Later Robbins admitted he was surprisingly impressed with the route—that it featured some of the hardest nailing he'd ever done. He also acknowledged being wrong in his desire to "erase" the route, calling his initial plan to do so a mistake. Said Robbins after the ascent: "Although this climb may not have been done exactly to our taste, and although we might have fretful little criticisms that envy always produces, we can better spend our energy in ways other than ripping and tearing, or denigrating the accomplishments of others...."

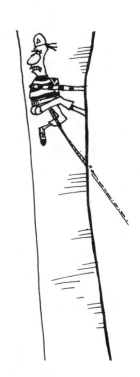

Footnotes

1 Achey, Jeff. "Path of the Elders," in *Climbing*, No. 186. Carbondale, CO: June 1999.

2 *Ibid.*

3 Twight, Marc F., and Martin, James. *Extreme Alpinism: Climbing Light, Fast, and High.* Seattle, WA: The Mountaineers, 1999.

4 Soles, Clyde. "The Mother of all Cam Charts," in *Rock & Ice*, No. 109. Boulder, CO: *Rock & Ice*, June/July 2001.

5 On the soft sandstone cliffs of eastern Germany's Elbsandstein near Dresden, the only removable protection leaders use are knotted slings wedged in tiny tunnels, or runners draped over natural horns and flakes. Because of the fragility of the rock, use of any metal protection is forbidden, a tradition that has been respected for years.

6 Soles, Clyde. "Camtasia," in *Rock & Ice*, No. 109. Boulder, CO: *Rock & Ice*, June/July 2001.

7 In 1971, the first guidebook to Yosemite Valley was published by Sierra Club Books. In this narrative guide, author Steve Roper denounces topos: "Designed to supplement or even replace the written description, topos are controversial in that they tend to make climbing a bit easier on the brain. Route-finding problems are simplified.... They encourage climbers onto difficult routes because of their unshakable belief in the topo.... Topos assure speed records; they also lessen responsibilty. No more querulous statements such as 'I'll just look around this corner,' only 'Here we are and where the hell's the belay bolt.' In other words, part of the adventure of climbing is removed. Topos are not used in this guidebook for the reasons mentioned above ...." Subsequent Yosemite guidebooks did eventually include topos, as do most modern guidebooks for other climbing areas today.

8   The late Jack Mileski, a climber who frequented the Shawangunks (The Gunks) in the early 1980s, was known for incessant shouting of instructions (spewing beta) from the ground to climbers on lead, whether they asked for suggestions or not. Verbosity proliferated at this popular upstate New York climbing area, even after Mileski moved to Colorado. Though Mileski has since died, his legacy of spewing beta reportedly lives on among locals at The Gunks.

9   A UIAA-rated fall involves 176 lbs falling 16´ on approximately 8´ of rope.

10 Twight, Marc. *Extreme Alpinism*.

11 Fasulo, David. *Self-Rescue*. Helena, MT: Falcon, 1996.

12 As an alternative, bring a few shoulder-length runners tied with accessory cord— these are more versatile because of their length.

13 For a left-handed brake, follow the same directions, but substitute left for right, and right for left.

Resources

Ament, Pat. *History of Free Climbing in America: Wizards of Rock.* Berkeley, CA: Wilderness Press, 2002.

Ament, Pat. *Royal Robbins: Spirit of the Age.* Lincoln, NE: Adventure's Meaning Press, 1992.

American Mountain Guides Association. *Technical Handbook for Professional Mountain Guides.* Golden, CO: AMGA, 1998.

Arce, Gary. *Defying Gravity—High Adventure on Yosemite's Walls.* Berkeley, CA: Wilderness Press, 1996.

Fasulo, David J. *Self-Rescue.* Helena, MT: Falcon, 1996.

Fyffe, Allen, and Peter, Iaian. *The Handbook of Climbing,* 2nd Edition. London: Pelham Books, 1997.

Graydon, Don and Hanson, Kurt, et al. (editors). *Freedom of the Hills,* 6th Edition. Seattle: WA: The Mountaineers, 1997.

Long, John. *Climbing Anchors.* Evergreen, CO: Chockstone, 1993.

Long, John. *Close Calls.* Helena, MT: Falcon, 1999.

Long, John. *How to Rock Climb,* 2nd Edition. Evergreen, CO: Chockstone, 1993.

Long, John, and Gaines, Bob. *More Climbing Anchors.* Evergreen, CO: Chockstone, 1996.

Long, John, and Luebben, Craig. *Advanced Rock Climbing.* Conifer, CO: Chockstone Press, 1997.

Luebben, Craig. *Knots for Climbers*. Helena, MT: Falcon, 1995.

MacDonald, Dougald, ed. *The Best of Rock & Ice Anthology*. Seattle, WA: The Mountaineers, 1999.

Millman, Dan. *The Warrior Athlete*. Walpole, NH: Stillpoint Publishing, 1979.

Robbins, Royal. *Advanced Rockcraft*. Glendale, CA: La Siesta Press, 1973.

Robbins, Royal. *Basic Rockcraft*. Glendale, CA: La Siesta Press, 1994.

Robinson, Doug. *A Night on the Ground, A Day in the Open*. La Crescenta, CA: Mountain N' Air Books, 1996.

Roper, Steve. *Camp 4—Recollections of a Yosemite Rockclimber*. Seattle, WA: The Mountaineers, 1994.

Roper, Steve, and Steck, Allen, editors. *The Best of Ascent*. San Francisco, CA: Sierra Club, 1993.

Roper, Steve; Steck, Allen; and, Harris, David, editors. *Ascent—The Climbing Experience in Word and Image*. Golden, CO: American Alpine Club, 1999.

Rowell, Galen A., ed. *The Vertical World of Yosemite: A Collection of Writings and Photographs on Rock Climbing in Yosemite*. Berkeley, CA: Wilderness Press, 1974.

Twight, Marc F., and Martin, James. *Extreme Alpinism: Climbing Light, Fast, and High*. Seattle, WA: The Mountaineers, 1999.

Glossary

acute mountain sickness (AMS): A non life-threatening condition occurring as low as 4,000' (1,250m) resulting from the body's adverse physiological reaction to an increase in altitude and barometric pressure, usually relieved by rest, light exercise, and hydration.

alpine climbing: Climbing in a high-altitude mountain environment involving the ascent of snow, ice, and rock. Sometimes referred to as mountaineering.

alpine start: A pre-dawn or early morning commencement of a climbing adventure.

anchor: A configuration of protection points to which climbers connect themselves with the rope for the purpose of belaying, rappelling, or top-roping.

artificial climbing: See direct-aid climbing.

ascenders: Mechanical devices used to ascend a fixed rope. See Jumars.

autoblock: One of several friction hitches that grip the rope when tightened and weighted. Also known as the French Prusik.

Bachman: A type of friction hitch rigged onto a carabiner. Like other friction hitches, the Bachman possesses gripping qualities that allows it to lock onto a rope when tightened and weighted.

back-clip: Erroneous clipping of the lead rope into a quickdraw carabiner so that if a fall occurs, the rope could open the gate of the carabiner and unclip itself.

back off: The act of retreating from a route.

backcountry: Remote site, usually in a wilderness setting, far from civilization.

backward zipper: During a lead fall, failure of several consecutive pieces of protection, closest to belayer beginning with the first piece and shifting to the next highest piece and so on.

belay: A backup safety system comprised of a rope, belayer, anchor, and belay device/method which allows a climber's fall to be halted. To belay is to manage such a system.

belay device: Device through which a climber's rope is threaded for the purpose of halting the rope by means of friction during a climber's fall.

belay escape: Initial self-rescue task requiring the tying off of a loaded rope leading to the victim so that the rescuer's hands are free, followed by a complete transfer of the load from rescuer to anchor if necessary. Once the escape is complete, the rescuer is free to conduct ensuing rescue activities.

belay plate: Friction belay/rappel device with a flat metal plate and an oblong hole.

belay stance or belay station: Anchor location.

belay tube: Tube-shaped belay/rappel device that relies on friction for braking.

belayer: The belay management role within a roped climbing partnership.

bergschrund: A large crevasse at the highest point of glacial activity, usually creating a formidable gap between the final approach and the base area of some alpine routes.

beta: Detailed route information regarding gear specifics, navigation, and/or movement sequences.

Big Bro: A spring-loaded tube-shaped device used to protect wide cracks.

big wall: A grade VI route in which the majority of climbing involves direct-aid.

bight: A loop (fold) of rope formed anywhere, of any size, between the rope's two ends.

bivouac (bivy): A night spent outdoors with minimal or no camping gear, sometimes unplanned.

bolt: A nail-like metal unit placed in a pre-drilled hole, usually by first-ascent parties, for use as a fixed protection point or anchor component. A permanent hanger, either pre-affixed or attached with a threaded nut, provides a clip-in point. Modern bolts are either secured into place by an expanding sleeve, or glue.

bomber: Completely secure and safe without question. From the term "bomb-proof".

bowline on a coil: A knot configuration that allows a non-harnessed climber to tie into the end of a rope.

carabiner: An aluminum alloy snap link with a spring-loaded gate used to connect various equipment components in a roped climbing ascent. Commonly known as a 'biner.

carabiner brake: Several carabiners clipped to a climber's harness assembled to create friction with threaded rope strand(s) for use as a rappel device.

chalk bag: Small cylindrical nylon container worn around a climber's waist to carry gymnast's chalk.

changeover: The process of gear exchange between the follower and the lead climber occurring at belay stations on multipitch routes.

chicken head: A narrow-necked rock protuberance with a broad, rounded head.

chock: See Stopper.

chockstone: A rock ranging in size from a pebble to a boulder, wedged in a crack or chimney.

class: A rating system of 1-5 developed by the Sierra Club which reflects terrain difficulty ranging from walking on a trail (1) to technical rock climbing requiring a rope and belay (5).

clean lead ascent: The description of a lead ascent in which no pitons are hammered into the rock for protection.

cleaning: The act of removing protection.

clove hitch: An adjustable hitch used for several purposes in climbing, most commonly to secure a rope into an anchor.

cold-shuts: Soft metal hook-like hardware units, sometimes hammered shut, pre-placed on the top of single-pitch routes and used for lowering climbers. Found mostly on sport climbs.

Comité European d'Normalisation (CEN): A European legislative body which oversees standards for climbing equipment used in industrial settings, and incidentally used also by recreational climbers.

counterweight rappel: An assisted rappel method used in self-rescue efforts in which the victim, tied to the end of the rope strand opposite the anchor from the rescuer, is lowered by the rescuer who manages the rappel device and simultaneously lowers him or herself.

cow's tail: A runner girth-hitched to a climber's harness and used as an anchor leash at belay or rappel stations.

crack: A rock crevice or fissure.

crack system: A series of continuous sections of cracks leading up a rock face.

crevasse: A deep and usually narrow ice fissure found on glacial terrain, often camouflaged by a layer of snow or ice.

crux: The single most difficult move or series of moves on a route.

daisy chain: An arm's length (approximately) strand of sewn webbing loops designed to be girth-hitched to a harness and used as an adjustable anchor leash at belay or rappel stations. Also used as an invaluable tool for aid climbers.

dihedral: Corner.

direct-aid climbing: A method of ascent used commonly on big walls in which climbers directly weight protection to obtain purchase for upward progress. Also known as direct-aid or artificial climbing.

double fisherman's knot: Knot commonly used to join the ends of rope, webbing, or cord. Also known as the grapevine knot.

double-rope leading: Rope technique involving the use of two ropes that can be clipped alternately to lead protection to prevent rope drag. Especially advantageous on meandering routes.

dynamic belay: Force-reducing technique in which the belayer deliberately allows slippage of a small amount of rope through the belay device during a lead fall.

epic: Common term for a climbing incident that evolves into a time-consuming, and sometimes dangerous episode.

escape route: An alternate course of travel allowing climbers to retreat or take a detour from originally intended route with relative ease.

étrier: A webbing "ladder" with several loops used as rungs to stand in during aid climbing ascents.

face: A relatively unbroken, featureless rock wall void of cracks. Also, general term for a large expanse of rock.

fall factor: Fall severity rating determined by the length of the fall and the amount of rope in use at the time of the fall.

figure-eight belay devices: Friction rappel device with two joined metal rings, one larger than the other.

figure-eight follow-through: One of the most common knots used to tie the rope into a harness. Also known as the rewoven Figure-eight.

figure-eight on a bight: Knot predominantly used for clipping into an anchor.

fixed gear: Pre-placed, non-removable gear usually left deliberately for other climbers to use. Includes (but not limited to) bolts and pitons.

flat overhand: Knot used to join the ends of two like-diameter ropes in rappel scenarios in which a low-profile knot is advantageous.

follow: The act of climbing after the leader has ascended. May require the cleaning (removal) of protection. Also known as seconding.

follower: The role in a climbing partnership of the climber who *follows* a route. See also second.

free climbing: Unassisted roped climbing in which climbers rely solely upon their own strength to ascend.

free soloing: Climbing without a rope and protection

French free: Term used to describe lead tactics on free climbs in which protection is overtly weighted and used as hand- or footholds to assist in making upward progress.

gear sling: A padded loop of webbing designed for carrying climbing hardware, worn over one shoulder and diagonally across the chest.

girth hitch: A simple hitch used to connect two loops of webbing or cord.

grade: A general route rating that loosely reflects a climb's length and technical difficulty.

grapevine knot: See double fisherman's knot.

GriGri: Trade name of a belay device that relies on a spring-loaded cam that grips the rope for automatic braking. Popularized at indoor climbing gyms and outdoor sport climbing settings.

ground-up: An ascent style in which climbers place all gear on lead opposed to establishing pre-placed protection points via rappelling from above. Used primarily to describe first-ascents.

hang-dogging: Resting on gear between difficult moves or utilizing passive gear to assist upward progress on free climbs.

hanging belay: A belay station void of any stances or ledges.

haul loop: A small sewn loop on a harness, pack, or other object used for clipping into a rope with a carabiner.

Hexcentric: Trade name for a hexagonal-shaped passive protection device designed to either wedge or cam into a crack. Known commonly as a Hex and manufactured by Black Diamond.

High Altitude Cerebral Edema (HACE):
A serious, life-threatening form of altitude illness resulting from the body's adverse reaction to an increase in altitude and barometric pressure in which fluid collects around the victim's cerebrum (brain). Occurring at altitudes as low as 8,000' (2,500m) but more common at much higher altitudes, HACE treatment requires immediate descent.

High Altitude Pulmonary Edema (HAPE):
A serious, life-threatening form of altitude illness resulting from an increase in barometric pressure in which fluid seeps out of pulmonary capillaries and begins to fill the alveolar spaces in the lungs. Occurring at altitudes of 8,000' (2,500m) and above, HAPE treatment requires immediate descent.

hip belay: An old-school belay method used prior to belay devices that relies upon friction created by wrapping the rope around the hips or buttocks for braking.

hueco: A rounded, concave rock feature varying in sizes. Translates as "hole" in Spanish.

ice climbing: An aspect of alpine climbing (mountaineering) involving the ascent of terrain consisting primarily of ice using crampons and ice axes.

impact force: The maximum force upon a rope that holds a fall. This amount is determined primarily

by fall factor and the falling climber's weight, but is also affected by varying degrees of friction within the system.

impact impulse: During a fall, the length of time over which energy is generated and dissipated throughout all the components of a roped climbing system. The longer the fall, the greater the impulse impact.

jamming: The insertion and downward torque of a hand, finger, foot, or toe for the purpose of obtaining purchase in a crack.

Jumars: Trade name for a specific brand of mechanical ascending devices. See ascending device.

Klemheist: Friction hitch with gripping qualities that allows it to lock onto a rope when tightened and weighted. From the German word "Klemme," meaning to clamp or jam.

leading/leader: A method of ascent in which a roped climber (the leader) moves up the rack while occasionally placing protection (hardware) or securing fixed gear into which the rope, payed out by a belayer from below, is clipped enroute to an anchor location above, no further than the length of the rope.

load-limiter: Any force-absorbing component of a roped climbing system used to reduce fall forces on equipment. See Yates' Screamer.

locker: A carabiner with a locking gate.

manky: Old, deteriorating, unreliable, unstable, sketchy, unsafe.

masterpoint: The final, primary link of an anchor where all individual anchor components are joined. The location on a multi-component anchor where climbers either thread the rope for rappelling or top-roping, or clip into at belays.

mountaineering: See alpine climbing.

mule knot: Knot commonly used in self-rescue scenarios to tie off a loaded rope or cord.

multipitch: Description of a climbing route longer than the length of one rope, requiring multiple belays.

Munter belay: A Munter hitch used in combination with a locking carabiner as a substitute belay device.

Munter mule knot: A knot combination consisting of a Munter hitch locked off with a mule knot, commonly used in self-rescue scenarios because it can be easily released under load.

nut: See Stopper.

nut tool: Thin, narrow metal pick used to extract Stoppers (nuts). Also known as a "nut key" or "cleaning tool".

off-route: A climbing team's unintentional detour from originally desired course of travel.

off-width: A crack too large for a fist or cupped-hand jam, but too small to enter and climb as a chimney.

on-sighting: Lead ascent in which the leader, having never climbed or viewed the climb before, ascends it without the aid of beta.

oppositional placement: Two pieces of protection set to withstand a force from opposing directions, linked together taut with a clove hitched runner. Used commonly in vertical cracks when both downward and lateral forces are possible.

overhand on a bight: Multi-purpose knot mostly used as a substitution for the Figure-eight on a bight although slightly inferior in security.

pendulum: A lateral, swinging fall. Also, an aid climbing technique used to swing laterally on an anchored rope to move from one crack system to another.

pitch: The distance between two belays not to exceed (usually) the length of the rope.

piton: A heavy metal peg hammered into cracks and crevices for use as lead protection or an anchor component. Most commonly used today on big walls, but also found fixed on some free climbs, many of which at one time were aid routes. Also referred to as a "pin".

primary link: A key link in any climbing system that without intentionally created redundancy, has no back-up. Two examples include the masterpoint of an anchor, and the carabiner linking a climber's harness to his or her belay/rappel device.

protection: General term referring to a piece of climbing hardware or a runnered natural feature (rock, tree, etc.) used as a component of an anchor, or intermittently for security by lead climbers. Free climbing protection is either "fixed" (bolts), or removable (SLCDs, Stoppers, Hexes, etc.) Pitons are removable, but are sometimes permanent. Also known as "pro".

Prusik: Friction hitch with gripping qualities that allow it to lock onto a rope when tightened and weighted.

quickdraws: Short versions of runners (slings), sewn or folded into lengths generally ranging from 3 to 12" (7.5-30cm). Originally a trade name, but now used a common reference to such runners.

rack: A wide assortment of climbing protection, runners, and carabiners used for creating anchors and setting protection on lead. Usually organized on a gear sling worn over one shoulder and diagonally across the chest, or on the leader's

waist attached to harness gear loops.

rap-bolting: A first ascent method involving the placement of bolts as protection points via rappeling from above.

rappel: Self-controlled descent of a rope that allows a descending climber to lower by feeding rope through a small friction device connected to his or her harness. Commonly referred to as an "abseil" outside the US. Prior to devices, climbers relied upon the classic Dulfersitz rappel method: friction was achieved by wrapping the rope around one thigh, up across the chest, and down across the back. Painful, insecure, but nevertheless effective.

rappel device: A metal device that creates friction enabling climbers to descend a fixed rope by lowering themselves. Common examples include tube, plate, and figure-eight devices.

rappel ring: An aluminum alloy ring usually found on rappel anchors and used as the masterpoint through which the rope is threaded.

rappel station: An established anchor site used for rappeling.

red-point: Final unassisted lead ascent of a route tried previously by a climber who fell or hung. Often completed after extensive preparation and rehearsal.

ring bend: Knot commonly used to join the ends of webbing or utility cord. Also known as the tape knot or water knot.

rope drag: Rope tension felt by a lead climber usually created by inadequate runnering that prevents the rope from running plumb between leader and belayer.

run it out: The placing of very little lead gear, either by choice, or as dictated by the absence of protection options.

runner: A multi-purpose nylon webbing loop, tied or sewn together, used in numerous applications to link two system components together and/or extend the distance between them. Alternately referred to as a sling. Also, the act of using a runner by a lead climber to reduce rope drag and torque on a protection point: "Be sure to runner (sling) the piece of protection you place under the roof."

runout: Term used to describe a leading scenario in which the distance between two pieces of protection is relatively far. Also used to describe a route or section of a route with few protection opportunities.

sandbag: Route that is more difficult than its given rating. Also, to indicate that a route is easier than it actually is.

second: The role in a climbing partnership of the climber who ascends after the leader. May require the cleaning (removal) of protection. Also known as the follower.

secondary link: Any redundant link in a climbing system.

seracs: Towers and blocks of ice in an ice fall posing potential hazards for the alpine climber.

SERENE: Common mnemonic used to remember five key elements of a good anchor:

> S=Safe/Secure;
> E=Equalized;
> R=Redundant;
> E=Easy;
> NE=No Extension.

sew it up: The activity of placing an abundance of lead protection.

shake out: To pause deliberately while climbing to shake arms in a downward fashion, usually one at a time, to achieve increased blood flow to overexerted muscles.

sharp end: Literally, the end of the rope to which a leader ties. Generally, a slang term used to describe the role and responsibilities of a lead climber. For example: "On the second pitch, she had no choice but to take the sharp end when her partner became ill."

shelf: On a pre-equalized cordelette anchor, an alternate clip-in site located directly above the masterpoint knot, incorporating one strand from each protection component.

shock-load: Sudden, direct loading of a piece of protection usually resulting from failure of another piece of equipment.

SLCD: See spring-loaded camming device

sling: See runner.

smearing: Climbing technique in which the ball and toes of the foot are placed flat against a rock wall as the climber simultaneously stands and weights the foot in an effort to create maximum friction to allow a temporary stance.

splitter: A smooth, parallel-sided crack, usually of significant length.

sport climbing: Term widely used to describe free climbing on bolted routes, in which gear placement is secondary to the primary focus of executing difficult moves. Most sport climbs ascend rock faces void of removable protection opportunities and are protected generously by bolts placed by first-ascent parties usually via rappel.

spring-loaded camming device (SLCD): A removable, spring-loaded device used for protection and anchoring. The SLCD, or camming device, has either three or four individual cam components which can be retracted by a trigger to fit into a cracks within its size range.

stemming: Climbing technique involving the use of the feet to create opposing force with between two distant footholds or walls.

Stopper™: A trade name for a wedging unit with tapered sides designed to slot into cracks and crevices for use as removable protection. Stoppers are referred to as passive protection because they have no movable parts. Also known as nuts, chocks, and tapers.

tandem rappel: Assisted rappel used in self-rescue efforts in which two climbers are attached with slings of different lengths to one rappel device, but only the lower individual has control of the brake line.

taper: See Stopper.

testpiece: A notoriously difficult route relative to its rating and other routes with similar ratings.

top-roping: Climbing protected by a rope that leads from the climber up to an anchor. A roped climbing system (known as a yo-yo or slingshot) in which the rope is threaded through a pre-established anchor at the top of a route and the belayer, situated at the base, takes in rope as the climber ascends.

traditional (trad) free climbing: Term widely used to describe a free-climbing style involving ground-up lead techniques with an emphasis upon placement of removable protection using existing options such as natural rock features and cracks.

trail line: A second rope trailed by either the leader or more commonly, the follower, used for rappel descents, hauling a pack, and/or as a backup for unplanned retreats.

Tri-Cam: Trade name for an unusually shaped protection device designed to passively cam or wedge into a crack. Designed by Lowe.

topo: Renderings of climbing routes indicating terrain specifics, distance, and sometimes technical information. From the word "topographical".

Union Internationale Associations d'Alpinisme (UIAA): An international mountaineering organization which helps govern the standards of climbing equipment.

Web-O-lette™**:** A 10 to 20′ strand of Spectra webbing featuring a sewn loop at both ends, created and manufactured by Mountain Tools for use in creating pre-equalized belay anchors.

webbing: Narrow strands of nylon material used to create items including runners (slings), harnesses, and quickdraws. Sold in most retail climbing shops from bulk spools.

whipper: A lead fall, usually unexpected and long.

Yates' Screamer™**:** A specialized quickdraw made by Yates' Gear with stitching designed to rip under force for the purpose of absorbing force created by a leader fall, and ultimately reducing force on equipment. (See loadlimiter.)

Yosemite Decimal System (YDS): The predominant rock climbing rating system today in North America, originating from the Sierra Club's Class rating system as an extension of Class 5.

Z-rig: A common rescue system used to create a mechanical advantage to raise an incapacitated climber.

Index

Author Note

Heidi Pesterfield lives in the Northern Sierra in Truckee, California, where for five years she has been a rock climbing instructor for Alpine Skills International (ASI). Her personal climbing adventures span nearly 20 years, 18 of which involve leading traditional routes. She has climbed throughout the United States, as well as in Italy and France.

Heidi is a professional member of the American Mountain Guides Association (AMGA), and recently completed her first AMGA instructor course. She is also a certified Wilderness First Responder (WFR). With a degree in journalism, Heidi has been a freelance writer for 17 years. She has published outdoor adventure articles in numerous magazines including *Climbing, Rock & Ice, City Sports, Summit*, and *Natural Health*. She also works closely with the Outdoor Industry Association (OIA) formerly Outdoor Recreation Coalition of America (ORCA), and is a frequent reporter for the *Daily Exposure*, at the biannual Outdoor Retailer Markets.

The idea for writing this book came to Heidi several years ago when she noticed a resurgent interest in traditional methods at her home crags of Donner Summit. "Sport climbers and top-ropers were watching trad climbers and saying 'I want to do *that*,'" she re-

members. ASI clients were requesting book recommendations on tradition lead craft, but, to her surprise, there wasn't one solely addressing these methods. She found chapters in several books and a video, but not one title devoted to leading trad free climbs. Her own learning years were a school of hard knocks, she recalls with a shudder. "It was trial and error, and I'm truthfully surprised I survived it. Had I access to a book like this I could have avoided a lot of risks."

Heidi enjoys climbing moderate, multipitch free routes in the High Sierra, as well as visiting different areas throughout the world. She likes sport climbing occasionally, but admits her passions lie with traditional methods. "You can't beat the exhilaration and adventure woven into the trad experience. And if you stick with it long enough, it'll take you to some of the most beautiful places on the planet."

SUPERTOPO Climbing Guides
From Wilderness Press

SuperTopo guides are essential for Yosemite climbers, with a perfect mix of history and strategy, ultra-detailed routes, and great color photos. Climbing expert and SuperTopo author Chris McNamara includes climbs with exceptional rock quality, elegant lines, fabulous views of the park, and fascinating history. The routes are especially appealing to Yosemite newcomers, but climbers of all experience and ability will enjoy them.

SuperTopo guides include everything a climber needs to know:
- Unbeatably accurate topos, including pitch lengths and gear sizes
- Route history and stories of colorful climbing pioneers
- Strategy, retreat, and storm information for each route
- Detailed approach and descent maps

Yosemite Ultra Classics

$14.95
80 pages, 6 x 9, softbound

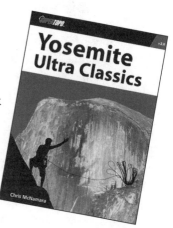

Yosemite boasts a mind-blowing selection of rock climbing opportunities. Yosemite Ultra Classics provides SuperTopos for 36 of the best classic climbs, most in the 5.4 to 5.10 range. In addition to classic Yosemite multi-pitch routes, this pack of SuperTopos includes climbs you can top-rope, and a section on how to master Yosemite crack climbing.

Tuolumne Ultra Classics

$14.95
72 pages, 6 x 9, softbound

Sharp, angular cracks, endless fields of knobs and golden glacier polish and spectacular granite peaks characterize climbs in the Tuolumne Meadows area—one of the finest collections of moderate alpine routes anywhere. *Tuolumne Ultra Classics* provides SuperTopos for 20 climbs in the 5.4 to 5.10 range. Few of these routes are easy (in Tuolumne there are few easy routes); most are moderately difficult with solid protection.

A History of Free Climbing in America

Wizards of Rock

PAT AMENT

$24.95
400 pages, 8½ x 11, softbound, illustrated

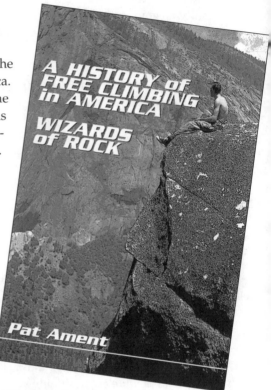

This is the definitive book about the free-climbing history of North America. While other books have covered some of this material, there has never been as clear a chronology or as thorough, accurate, and well-researched a treatment. Pat Ament, a world-class climber himself, leaves the critique and analysis to others and lets these remarkable events speak for themselves in a succinct, refreshing, and inimitable style.

A History of Free Climbing in America includes interviews with, and commentary by, many world-class climbers, including Royal Robbins, John Gill, Pete Cleveland, Henry Barber, John Bachar, Lynn Hill, John Long, Steve Roper, Jimmy Dunn, Dean Potter, Alan Watts, and many others. Photographs from prominent climbing photographers, such as Tom Frost, accent the book. Art work by the author further illustrate the prose and bring to life the dynamic personalities of the climbing world.

The book covers the Adirondacks in upstate New York, Arizona, the Pacific Northwest, Devils Lake in Wisconsin, The Needles in South Dakota, Yosemite, and many more destinations.

Call or email to place your order today!

Wilderness Press
Toll free: (800) 443-7227
Fax: (510) 558-1696
email: mail@wildernesspress.com